# HOTLY IN PURSUIT OF THE REAL

# HOTLY IN PURSUIT OF THE REAL

*Notes Toward a Memoir*

## Ron Hansen

HOTLY IN PURSUIT OF THE REAL
Notes Toward a Memoir

Slant
An Imprint of Wipf and Stock Publishers
199 W. 8th Ave., Suite 3
Eugene, OR 97401

www.wipfandstock.com

HARDCOVER ISBN: 978-1-5326-9203-1
PAPERBACK ISBN: 978-1-5326-9202-4
EBOOK ISBN: 978-1-5326-9204-8

*Cataloguing-in-Publication data:*

Names: Hansen, Ron.

Title: Hotly in pursuit of the real : notes toward a memoir / Ron Hansen.

Description: Eugene, OR: Slant, 2020

Identifiers: ISBN 978-1-5326-9203-1 (hardcover) | ISBN 978-1-5326-9202-4
(paperback) | ISBN 978-1-5326-9204-8 (ebook)

Subjects: LCSH: Novelists, American—20th century—Biography | Christianity
and literature—United States | Christian biography—United States | Fiction—
Authorship

Classification: PS33558.A5133 H68 2020 (paperback) | PS33558.A5133 (ebook)

Manufactured in the U.S.A.                                        04/18/19

*To Bo—ever my first reader*

# CONTENTS

# PREFACE

EVEN AS A HIGH SCHOOL STUDENT MY FICTIONS WERE NOT ABOUT ME. I tilted toward what Edgar Allan Poe called "Arabesques," or what others might consider tales from *The Twilight Zone*. I didn't find my life interesting enough, so I invented. Of course, what I'd experienced or read or overheard influenced my scenes and sometimes my dialogue, but family and friends would be hard-pressed to find themselves inside what I wrote. Everything was disguised. Writing for me was very close to acting, each role a fleshing out, yet finding something of myself in each.

In high school and college, I closely examined and learned from John Updike and his domestic, realistic, New England stories, but I did not at all imitate him. In graduate school at the University of Iowa's Writers' Workshop, my primary instructor, a young John Irving, whose family I lived with as *au pair* for his boys, taught me how to healthily live the novelist's life, but I am far from writing like John or following his path, alas. And that goes for John Gardner or John L'Heureux or any others who've counseled me in my work. It's rather odd to feel so indebted to past teachers and yet find yourself not at all like them except in still choosing to not write autobiographically.

I seem to have followed Gustave Flaubert who advised, "Be regular and ordinary in your life so that you may be violent and original in your work." I live in the suburbs across from the main headquarters of Apple; I generally go to the gym each day and play golf about once a week; I go to Mass rather often; I drive a BMW coupe; our daughter and son lead normal, admirable lives; my novelist wife Bo and I watch sitcoms on the sofa at night, our Labrador gnawing a bone between us. We're as conventional as they come. Laughing at the incongruity of a fiction writer in such a high-tech and seemingly unromantic a place, a journalist once called me "the bard of Cupertino."

Although I'm still cautious about it, in my essays I'm more public. My life story leaks through. A topic or question is presented by an editor or institution, and like a hungry, earnest, eager-to-please graduate student I launch into the writing with faint hopes of final success and with some inchoate thoughts that, with luck, ever so gradually congregate and become a fixed point of view that is illustrated by my own history. Even when I think of myself as hidden, the curtain fully drawn, I am, more than in my fiction, fully present with my cranky opinions, my perhaps varnished memories, my *sui generis* predilections.

E. M. Forster wrote, "How do I know what I think until I see what I say?" And so it is with my essays. Writing about becoming a novelist, my reflections fly to the past and a childhood that took me fully by happenstance toward that peculiar occupation. Writing about the gift of awareness, I first go to the comments of Simone Weil. When asked to write about heretics, I recall the life of the Jesuit George Tyrell. No matter the subject, each paragraph begins with the haunting question "What shall I say next?" and that jogs memories and opinions I was not particularly alert to.

And so in the reflections that follow I offer readers more overt glimpses of myself, my loved ones, my heroes, hobbyhorses, and obsessions. Whether I ever write a memoir isn't yet certain, but these snapshots are at least a start.

I

# HOTLY IN PURSUIT OF THE REAL

EVER SINCE I LEARNED TO READ, I HAVE WANTED TO BE A FICTION writer. The vocation was nascent at first, for books seem as authorless as rain to a child, but it insisted that I not only inhabit the world imagined by others, as good readers do, but go on with the story, configure it to fit my own life, filch it like candy left out in a bowl. Robert Coles names this odd hankering and delight "the call of stories."

I may have been five or so when I first noticed that calling. At Sunday Mass in Omaha, the priest ascended the stairs to the high pulpit at Holy Angels Church, announced a reading from one of the Gospels, and after a few sentences of the passage I was suddenly aware that the story was familiar to me. Say it was the shockingly concrete scene in Mark where Jesus heals a blind man by wetting the man's eyes with his spittle. I found myself anticipating the next moves, certain that the man would say he could see people but they looked like trees walking. And Jesus would lay his hands on the afflicted man's eyes again, and then the man would see everything clearly. The sentences were sure and predictable to me; I felt I was finally their audience, and I realized with a good deal of wonder that the Gospels were like those children's books that my mother or sisters would read to me over and over again. With great seriousness the priest would read aloud the meaning of the passage in our own lives, and even the old in the congregation would watch and listen like children being taught.

The liturgical rites were grand theater then, filled with magisterial ceremony, great varieties of mystery and symbol and a haunting Gregorian chant that sounded lovely even if poorly sung. And since I could not yet follow the English translation of the priest's Latin in my missal, I would fix my gaze high overhead on the soft blue sky of the dome, on which there was a huge, literal, and beautiful painting of Christ being escorted by the holy angels on his ascension to heaven, his loose white clothing floating off him so that most of his flesh was exposed.

Looking back on my childhood now, I find that church-going and religion were in good part the origin of my vocation as a writer, for along with Catholicism's feast for the senses, its ethical concerns, its insistence on seeing God in all things and the high status it gave to scripture, drama and art, there was a connotation in Catholicism's liturgies that story-telling mattered. Each Mass was a narrative steeped in meaning and metaphor, helping the faithful not only to remember the past but to make it present here and now and to bind ourselves into a sharing group so that, ideally, we could continue the public ministry of Jesus in our world.

On the other hand, my vocation as a writer was also called forth by something unnamable that I can only associate with a yen to live out in my imagination other lives and possibilities, a craving that eventually made acting attractive to my brother Rob and soon made storytelling necessary to me.

In kindergarten, for example, we had an afternoon period of show-and-tell. A few minutes earlier, a boy named Kenneth breathlessly told me about the side altar at some European cathedral his family had visited, where a pressure-sensitive prie-dieu illuminated a crucifix when penitents fell on their knees to pray. Seeing my fascination, five-year-old Kenneth confused the scene and himself with flashing colors and whirring mechanisms that seemed lifted from a science-fiction movie. I fell into my own imagining as Sister Martha went from child to child, asking them to report on adventures, discoveries, encounters or anything else they thought noteworthy. And then she got to me.

I instinctively said a neighbor had turned a hallway closet into a chapel, with holy pictures everywhere, and there were lots of candles burning all the time, and there was a kneeler in front of a crucifix and when you knelt on it, real blood trickled out of the wounds in Christ's hands and feet. Real blood? Sister Martha asked. Well, it looked like real blood, it was red like blood, and it trickled down his face from the crown of thorns, too. She squinted at me with just a twitch of a smile, and I was shocked, even insulted that she could think I was making this up. Hadn't I seen that hallway closet, that padded prie-dieu, that crucifix with my own eyes? I could describe the finest detail; I could smell the candle wax as it burned. Stifling her amusement, the kindergarten teacher questioned me more closely, possibly having found a kids-say-the-darndest-things instance that she could present like chocolate pie to her sisters at dinner, and I just kept embellishing and filling in gaps in the narrative until Sister Martha seemed to decide I was depleted and she shifted to another child. And when I looked at Kenneth, he was wide-eyed and in awe, with no hint of affront for my having stolen his show and tell, but with a certain amount of jealousy that I'd seen a prie-dieu that was so far superior to his and, worse, seemed to have tried to selfishly keep it to myself.

Within the year I would be reading on my own and finding out about children's books and children's authors and their need to do just what I did: to alter facts that seemed imposed and arbitrary, to intensify scenes and situations with additions and falsifications and to ameliorate the dull and slack commodities of experience with the zest of the wildest imaginings.

The first author whose name I remembered and whose stories I hunted down was Jules Verne, whom I avidly read in the third grade. In fourth grade it was Albert Payson Terhune—I even named our foundling pup after his "Lad"—and *Peck's Bad Boy*, by Aurand Harris, with its gladdening irony that a boy who was continually getting into trouble with grownups might simply be just acting like boys do. Then it was fifth grade and the Hardy Boys and Tom Swift, books meant for kids my age but that seemed hopelessly old-fashioned and did not thrill me nearly so much as the tales of Edgar Allan Poe, who so hooked me that I held his book of horror stories open in my lap to sneak peeks at as I pretended to take classroom notes. I was drawing and painting then, not writing fiction. A friend's father was an illustrator and I fantasized that I would have a job like that when I got out of school. But gradually an urgency to write fiction took over; it was a vocation that seemed so exalted and sacred and beyond me I would not even talk about it.

In "Confessions of a Reluctant Catholic," the novelist Alice McDermott recalls learning to be a writer, which "seemed to me from the outset to be an impossible pursuit, one for which I had no preparation or training, or even motive, except for a secret and undeniable urge to do so." She had discovered that "fiction made the chaos bearable; fiction transformed the absurdity of our brief lives by giving context and purpose and significance to every gesture, every desire, every detail. Fiction transformed the meaningless, fleeting stuff of daily life into the necessary components of an enduring work of art."

The intuition of the fiction writer is similar to that of the scientist: that the world is governed by rules and patterns that are, by analysis and experiment, detectable; that the hidden mysteries of nature can be interrogated and solved. I have run into people who don't read fiction because they feel it is founded on fabrications and swindles and worthless extenuations of reality—professional golfer John Daly once complained about the English classes he took in college, where he was forced to read "these big, fat books that weren't even true"—but for many of us fiction holds up to the light, fathoms, simplifies, and refines those existential truths that, without such interpretation, seem all too secret, partial, and elusive.

And that, of course, is the goal of religion as well. Some writers are agnostic and have as their religion art, but just as many are conscious that the source of their gifts is God and have found thanksgiving, worship, and praise of the Holy Being to be central to their lives and artistic practice. In *An American Requiem: God, My Father, and the War That Came Between Us*, James Carroll wrote that "the very act of story-telling, of arranging memory and invention according to the structure of narrative is, by definition, holy." And in a later interview Carroll stated that "my notion of narrative informs my faith, and my notion of faith informs my idea of what writing is for."

Writing gives form and meaning to our sometimes disorderly existence. It gives the author the chance for self-disclosure and communion with others, while also giving readers a privileged share in another's inner life that, perhaps imperceptibly, questions and illuminates our own. Reading attentively, connecting our lives with those of fictional characters, choosing ethically and emotionally just as they do or in contradistinction to them, we enter the realm of the spirit where we simultaneously discover our likeness to others and our difference, our uniqueness. Questioning ourselves and our world, finding in it, for all its coincidence, accidents, and contingencies a mysterious coherence, we may become aware of a horizon beyond which abides the One who is the creator and the context of our existence.

Writing on the Catholic short-story master Andre Dubus, Tobias Wolff noted that in his friend's work "the quotidian and the spiritual don't exist on separate planes, but they infuse each other. His is an unapologetically sacramental vision of life in which ordinary things participate in the miraculous, the miraculous in ordinary things. He believes in God, and talks to him, and doesn't mince words. He is open to mystery, and of all mysteries the one that interests him the most is the human potential for transcendence."

Edifying Christian fiction can have a tendency to attenuate the scandal of the incarnation by circumscribing the sensual or sordid facts of the flesh in order to concentrate on heavenly actions and aspirations. And in doing so such fiction fails both the mysteries we are informed of by faith and those mysteries of sin and redemption we perceive in our daily lives. We need Christian fiction writers who are, in Flannery O'Connor's phrase "hotly in pursuit of the real." She noted that "the chief difference between the novelist who is an orthodox Christian and the novelist who is merely a naturalist is that the Christian novelist lives in a larger universe. He believes that the natural world contains the supernatural. And this doesn't mean that his obligation to portray nature is less; it means it is greater."

In an essay entitled "How to Be an American Novelist in Spite of Being Southern and Catholic," Walker Percy identified the inherent congeniality of Christianity to the vocation of the novelist

> The Christian ethos sustains the narrative enterprise in ways so familiar to us that they can be overlooked. It underwrites those very properties of the novel without which there is no novel: I am speaking of the mystery of human life, its sense of predicament, of something having gone wrong, of life as a wayfaring and a pilgrimage, of the destiny and linearity of time and the sacramental reality of things. The intervention of God in history through the Incarnation bestows a weight and value to the individual human narrative that is like money in the bank to the novelist. Original Sin is out of fashion, both with Christians and with Jews, let alone unbelievers. But any novelist who does not believe that his character finds himself in a predicament not entirely of his own making or of society's making is in trouble as a novelist. And any novelist who begins his novel with his character in a predicament which is a profound mystery and to which he devotes

his entire life to unraveling is a closet Jew or Christian whether he
likes it or not.

Even in high school it was my habit to send off my short stories to
magazines for possible publication. I was never very disappointed when
they were rejected, for I had no illusions that my callow stories were any
good, but I had never in my life met a fiction writer, and the profession
seemed so magnificent to me that my quest to try it seemed outlandish.
My regular submissions to magazines were messages in a bottle, ways of
keeping contact with a lovesick yearning that was gradually becoming my
soul's signature. And when I was a junior at Creighton, a short story that
was the first I felt proud of was rejected by The Atlantic Monthly with a
letter from the fiction editor gently indicating what the errors and holes
in that particular story were while generously urging me to send in something else.

I ought to have been gladdened by that letter, but instead I was de-
jected, because in spite of the editor's notes to me, the necessary skills and
discipline of revision were not yet mine, and I hadn't the slightest notion
of how to make my flawed and unfinished story any better than it was.
And I found myself wondering if I wasn't kidding myself about my talent
and wasting my time in a foolish and vainglorious pursuit.

Then a picture flashed in my mind for just a fraction of a second. It
was there and then, instantly, it was not. But I was sure that God had favored me with a foretaste of the future, for what I fleetingly glimpsed was
a page in a magazine like *Time* or *Newsweek* and a few inches of a column
that was indisputably a book review. I couldn't read the book's title or any
other words on that page, but I knew with rock-hard certainty that the
book being reviewed was by me. With that one look major questions were
answered, a critical juncture, perhaps, was passed, and I was flooded with
feelings of calm and bliss and purposefulness.

Writing on vocation in *Magister Ludi*, the great German novelist Herman Hesse noted, "There are many types and kinds of call, but the core of
the experience is always the same: your soul is awakened, transformed, or
exalted, so that instead of dreams and presentiments from within, a sum-
mons comes from without, a portion of reality presents itself and makes
a claim."

I have discovered in late night conversations that many of my friends have had profound experiences of God's hand, God's voice, God's solace, God's gentle invitation. But how often are those experiences written about? Yet they are as important, indelible, and real as anything else that happens to us. Catholic writers may principally differ from others in their heightened awareness of the unseen but ineluctable foundation of our existence, and in their unsqueamish and unembarrassed insistence that one is hotly in pursuit of the real, especially when writing about the substance of things hoped for.

# MAKING THINGS UP

IN ONE OF HIS COMIC MONOLOGUES ON THE *PRAIRIE HOME COMPANION* radio show, Garrison Keillor related:

> Well it's been a quiet week in Lake Wobegon, Minnesota, my hometown out there on the edge of the prairie. Most of the leaves are off the trees. . .of course the corn is all combined, the beans as well. The fields are mostly just stubble. . . . It's a November landscape, a reminder to all of us to look for our warm things, and to get ourselves a good windshield scraper. When a big storm comes in a week or two, you don't want to have to be scraping the ice off your windshield with your credit card. It would look like you weren't from here. It's a good time, winter, for all of us. It's a time when all the things that we've been postponing for months can now be put off a good while longer. . .All of those improvement projects, including self-improvement, those can all be put off until spring because winter brings us back to basics. We're back to survival now. Just back to the fundamentals: food and heat and of course the obligation that we all have to tell stories, which is why God put us here, after all. [That] is to live rich, full lives and then to tell about it, or better yet, to know other people who have lived rich, full lives and tell stories about them.

American mythologist Joseph Campbell called those stories we find ourselves telling "a cacophonous chorus" that originated with our primal ancestors exaggerating their heroism in hunting expeditions and speculating about the occult world that the spirits of slaughtered animals journeyed to after their deaths. In both oral and literate cultures, stories function to make coherent, expected, and tolerable the collective experiences of the people, whether those experiences be the negative ones of sickness, death, and conflict, or the happier products of marriage, child-birth, hunting and gathering, and making ends meet.

We all are fiction and poem makers even when we feel we're adhering closely to the historical record (which is itself, of course, a fiction: a thing shaped or made), for even in our narratives of a trip to the grocery store or our paeans on the glories of nature there are elements we heighten or shade or color. There are amendments, excuses, and subtractions, in-vented comments or things we wish we would have said, failures at full disclosure. And always there is *affect*, our feelings about what happened to us or to others.

But the need to fasten one's stories to a page and hand out one's col-lected pages to strangers is odd, and I have a little to say about the origins of that oddness.

***

One of my first childhood memories is a scene in the kitchen of our home on Fowler Street in Omaha. I was in my first year, in a highchair adjacent to my mother, and my twin brother Rob was in a highchair fac-ing her. At the far end of the kitchen table, sunlight filling the window behind her, was my sister Gini, seven years older than Rob and me, and notoriously antagonistic to vegetables of all sorts. My mother was spoon-feeding my brother and me something dark green from a Gerber's jar, possibly mashed peas or spinach, and Gini, holding back a grimace, asked her if the boys really liked that stuff. My mother said, "They seem to eat almost everything."

And I was struck, at the age of one, without of course comprehend-ing what I'd learned, that the English language had been a kind of wild snowstorm around me, but now, whether my sister or mother recognized it or not, I understood every word they said.

Half a century later, I found myself wondering why I so clearly re-membered that kitchen scene until at a dinner party a psychiatrist told me that language acquisition is the first step in the separation between children and their mothers. I had stamped in my mind a primal scene in which that differentiation became luminous.

Even now as I write this, I am joining you in our calling, our simi-larities, our joint aspirations, but I also am using these words, these verbal events, to fashion a new reality that wholly separates me from you. Writers seem to have a greater need than others to do that, but it seems to be hard-wired in humanity in general. To quote the British poet Gerard Manley Hopkins: "Each mortal being does one thing and the same: / ... *myself* it speaks and spells, / Crying *What I do is me: for that I came.*"

Rob and I worked out a language of our own, as many twins do. My father's father had made us a play table, so that we faced each other with our wooden blocks and toys, and my mother would duck her head into our bedroom to hear us happily chattering away in a vocabulary completely invented, and which we alone understood. When we were three or so, we were in the family car, heading to downtown Omaha and about to bump over the railroad tracks beside the Nabisco factory. I turned to Rob and said a word like "hoarhound," which meant "railroad train" to us and perhaps was a child's imitation of the wailing noise of a locomotive as it approached a crossroads.

My mother turned in the front seat of our car and asked with honest curiosity, "What does that word mean? You always say it here."

We both stared forward, saying nothing, gun-shy, and that was the last time I can remember speaking our invented language. I now have forgotten our secret vocabulary, and I regret it.

I have written elsewhere about being accidentally excluded from a kindergarten Christmas pageant. This was in Omaha, 1952.

Sister Josefina selected Cynthia Bash, the prettiest girl, to play Mary, and John Kocarnik, the tallest boy, got to play Joseph, choices I probably would have made if asked. But then three boys I found, at best, annoying were assigned the roles of Magi, whom I knew got to wear the fanciest costumes, and a handful of girls were joined into choirs of angels, and finally Rob and some troublemakers and oafs were handed the no-line jobs of shepherds. And that was it. My name had not been mentioned. Of all the kindergartners at Holy Angels Grade School, I was the only one without a role in the Christmas play.

I was afraid that I'd flunked kindergarten, as I'd seen some whiny and incontinent children do. Wanting to know for sure just how bad my situation was, I got the gumption to walk up to Sister Josefina at playtime and while fighting off tears told her she'd left me out. To my astonishment, she was not irritated with me. She seemed, instead, embarrassed.

She probably had intended to recite Luke's nativity story herself, but on seeing my worried face, she was inspired by pity to say, "Well, we'll need a narrator. You can be Saint Luke."

The last shall be first.

Classmates looked at me with stunned envy when I confided about it, and even my parents seemed impressed and surprised that Sister had honored me with such a hallowed role. My kindergarten friends were each given little scraps of paper on which their lines had been printed out in order to practice them aloud with someone who could read, but I handed over to my mother a full page of a Big-Chief tablet that was filled with handwriting I couldn't yet decipher.

We'd sit at the dining room table at night and she'd read a sentence from chapter 2 of Luke until I could accurately repeat it, and then she'd go on to another sentence. I have a sense of the great language acquisition gifts of children when I recall how little we actually practiced those lines before I had them fast in my head.

On the night of the Christmas pageant, as a hundred people found their seats on folding chairs, I stood off to the side in a turban made from one of my sister's pink towels and in my own striped bathrobe from home, but unfortunately without the filthy charcoal mustache and beard that my friends who were shepherds wore, so my pleasure was incomplete. While the kindergarten girls sang "O Little Star of Bethlehem," I saw my folks grinning hopefully at their twin sons, while my sister Gini frowned at me in a way that said, *Don't screw this up. I have friends here.* And then, with the song finished and Sister nodding me forward, I walked to the front of the audience and in the high scream of a five-year-old projecting his voice, I announced, "At that time, there went forth a decree from Caesar Augustus that a census of the whole world should be taken!"

On and on I went, reciting sentences I didn't fully understand. "And it came to pass while they were there, that the days for her to be delivered were fulfilled. And she brought forth her firstborn Son, and wrapped Him in swaddling clothes, and laid Him in a manger, because there was no room for them in the inn."

When I finished I felt Sister Josefina's relief that I hadn't forgotten anything, and I watched as my friends completed their histrionic

13

pantomime of star-gazing, childbirth, and adoration. The Magi sang, "We Three Kings of the Orient Are" and we all joined together on "Hark, the Herald Angels Sing," and then it was over and the families applauded their own.

I frequently have been asked when it was that I first had the impulse to be a fiction writer, and I find myself often thinking of that kindergarten play and of those hundred grown-ups and older children whom I knew weren't listening to me but to those fascinating and archaic words: *betrothed, swaddling, manger.* I felt the power that majestic language had for an audience, that they'd been held rapt not just because of what Luke and I reported but because of the way we said it.

My first-grade teacher was Sister Clida, a harried Dominican nun whose purgatory was here on earth in a classroom of thirty-two hyperactive children, some of whom were incompletely housebroken.

One afternoon Sister Clida taught us some basic arithmetic and introduced us to the concept of a quiz on the material she'd just covered. We were handed out half-sheets of lined paper and were supposed to solve the addition problems she'd chalked on the blackboard. Well, just the night before I had learned to fold a paper airplane, and that sleek craft yawing and banking in fluent flight seemed, to me, far more interesting than the resolution of the problem, *What is four plus two?*

When Sister Clida sidled down the cramped aisles of the classroom, collecting the quizzes, I handed over my paper airplane with such gleeful innocence that she thought at first it was sarcasm. Even when she saw it was not, she blew, as they say, a gasket. Fearing that she might do me harm, she took me by the hand and marched me across the hallway to the seventh-grade classroom. There the nun who was teaching accepted me with calm, and my sister Gini scowled as I smugly took a seat in a big kid's desk, my feet dangling, my folded arms as high as my chin on the writing table.

I could not understand anything the nun there was talking about, but I felt I'd scored a major victory and skipped six grades with that paper airplane. After an hour, when the older nun thought it safe, I was conveyed back to my first-grade class, and a pacified Sister Clida said nothing to me. I was happy, content, with zero remorse for my grand adventure—and getting away with that had more than a little to do with my becoming a fiction writer. The fiction I write seems to me merely grown-up versions of paper airplanes.

\*\*\*

Although I grew up in the large-ish city of Omaha, there were still pockets of agrarian culture and half a block from our house were corn fields, railroad tracks, and the Snell Sash & Door Company, where there were forts of wooden pallets and where empty, wonderfully available railway box cars waited for their freight. All these were ideal hang-outs for boys. We dug foxholes and patrolled for Nazis like the characters in *Combat*, ate wild mulberries and sunflower seeds, clambered all over those box cars, and had our pennies flattened on the rails by passing locomotives. Once a railroad detective caught us and sent my father a letter warning of the mortal dangers of doing what we were doing. My father tried to reprimand us, but we could tell his heart wasn't in it. Railroad tracks, he knew, were just too attractive to boys.

But gradually we got to an age when that make-believe world seemed like kids' stuff, even unmanly, and it was about then that a nun at Holy Angels assigned our religion class the written homework of an essay on the Crucifixion. I instinctively realized I didn't want to analyze it, or quote sources on it. I wanted to write about the Crucifixion as if I were actually there on Golgotha, and I have no idea why but I had the temerity to raise my hand and ask if an imaginative version would be permitted.

Sister Pierce seemed confused at first, but since I was the only kid who'd requested to write fiction instead of an essay, she didn't think it would be a problem. I produced a short story very much like Ernest Hemingway's very bad short play "Today Is Friday," which I hadn't yet read, about Roman soldiers who witnessed Jesus dying on the cross and speaking about it over grappa later on. Hemingway has a Roman soldier say in his playlet, "I tell you, he was pretty good in there today," and my own version was possibly just as anachronous and maudlin.

Sir Laurence Olivier was once asked how one could properly make a decision about a life in the theater, and he simply responded, "If anything can keep you from acting, let it."

There is a choicelessness in creative writing, too. And I had discovered in that Holy Angels classroom a fascinating, isolating, and still incipient need that seemed peculiar only to me: the yearning to make things up—essentially to improve on the life I had experienced either through reading or being knocked about as we all are. It was a kind of lying, but for the good of the characters, for the good of the audience.

In writing about his own poems in his book of essays, *The Glass Anvil*, Andrew Hudgins mentions the quandary poets and fiction writers face in making things up:

> I'm always astonished at how falsely I remember things, astonished at how plastic memory is. And even when I know a memory is incorrect, part of my brain cleaves to the wrong, imagined memory, and now I hold two images in my head, two memories—and the false one is more vivid and more emotionally significant to me than the actual one. Which, then, is the truest memory? It's convenient when the actual events adequately convey the emotional experience, but sometimes they don't and the writer has to choose.

Often the choice devolves to which version provides the juicier words, for crucial to the urge to write is a fascination with the English language that for me probably had its roots in the secret language Rob and I shared as twins. I recall one short story from my freshman year in Omaha's all-boys Jesuit high school—a kind of Rod Serling *Twilight Zone* thriller—only because I managed to fit the fancy, tailorish word "habiliment," rather than "clothing" into the story. And I recall one cartoon from our freshman-year vocabulary textbook. A little boy tells his mother, "We learned a new word in school today. Can you surmise what it is? I'll give you three surmises."

I was that kid.

Etymologies engrossed me, and one of my grander moments in high school occurred when in my illicit reading—a book open on my knees but hidden from my English teacher—I fell upon the word "onomatopoeia," which is defined as the formation of a word by imitation of the sound to which it refers, such as bang and boom. I couldn't remember ever having seen such a strange word before, so I puzzled over it for a while. The next thing I knew, our English teacher—a layman in his twenties named Mr. Schaeffer—was giving us our difficult weekend reading assignment. A classmate, Mickey Deising, complained that the weather was going to be beautiful and the homework hard. Couldn't Mr. Schaeffer let us off just this once? And the sporty teacher negotiated a deal with us: our class could pick one person, and the teacher could pick a word. If that student could spell it, we'd have no homework for the weekend.

You probably see where this is heading.

To my surprise and trepidation, the class picked me, chanting, "Hansen, Han-sen," and so I became the chosen one, and Mr. Schaeffer, already clearly complacent about his victory, chose the most difficult word he knew. "All right, Mr. Hansen," he said. "Spell onomatopoeia."

I couldn't believe my luck, and when I correctly spelled the word, Mr. Schaeffer loudly said "Shit!" and the classroom erupted in wild hoots and cheers.

\*\*\*

At age sixteen I was given a summer job as an assistant greenskeeper on a nine-hole golf course, hosing off the dew the first thing each morning, mowing the greens, then resetting the cups and pins. I hated my ignorant, racist, ex-con of a boss but I loved the outdoor, barefoot, shirtless work, and a nice plus turned out to be that I was home before three in the afternoon with nothing to do but read. Suntanned a mahogany shade and still in my jean shorts and tee-shirt, I once wandered into Kenwood Drugstore after work on the golf course and turned the metal paperback rack until I fell upon John Updike's novel *The Centaur*. And reading the praise on its jacket, I felt a spasm of good sense and bought it.

Interweaving aspects of the Greek myth of Chiron, the wise centaur that taught Achilles, Asclepius, and others, with autobiographical fragments about the kindly schoolteacher George Caldwell in a small Pennsylvania town in the 1940s, *The Centaur* was an intelligent, experimental, classically-inspired novel about a father-son relationship that was also so gorgeously written that it won the National Book Award for its author at the age of thirty-one.

Updike's intent, he once said, was "to give the mundane its beautiful due." My enthusiasms in grade school had been located on the grotesque and arabesque, on Jules Verne, Edgar Allan Poe, and a World War II memoir, *Back to Bataan*, which is the first book I can recall rereading immediately after I'd finished it. But in John Updike I found the exact writer I wanted to be. And it was John Updike who later noted in his essay "Religion and Literature" that the English Victorians generally wrote with the presumption of a religious sensibility on the part of their readers, but that the modernists—responding to the wreckage of conviction wrought by Darwin, Freud, and Marx—sought to make art itself their religion. And so the twentieth century became, for many, an age of disbelief. Updike wrote:

> Yet it remains curiously true that the literary artist, to achieve full ef-fectiveness, must assume a religious state of mind—a state that looks beyond worldly standards of success and failure. A mood of exalta-tion should possess the language, a vatic tension and rapture. Even a grimly tragic view, like that of King Lear, Samuel Beckett, Céline, and Herman Melville, must be expounded with a certain rapt celebra-tive air. The work of literary art springs from the world and adheres to it but is distinctly different in substance. We enter it, as readers, expecting an intensity and shapeliness absent in our lives. A realm above nature is posed—a supernatural, in short. Aesthetic pleasure, like religious ecstasy, is a matter of inwardness, elevation, and escape.

Writing a bestseller would be welcome but was never an important goal for me. Writing a good story was, and still is. Were I not financially rewarded for my writing, I'm certain I would continue making things up even if I were, like Emily Dickinson or Franz Kafka or Gerard Manley Hopkins, writing only for a few choice friends. There is joy in the simple making of things, for creativity, as Ignatius of Loyola pointed out, is a par-ticipation in the divine.

***

Consider that famous gospel statement in John 3:16. In the King James Bible translation it is: "For God so loved the world, that he gave his only begotten Son, that whosoever believeth in him should not perish, but have everlasting life."

Consider that opening phrase: "For God so loved the world." There are aspects of our world that we can repudiate and even despise, but our foremost commitment as people of faith is to find and give description to those aspects of his creation that God so loves.

The Pulitzer Prize-winning poet Galway Kinnell once said, "To me, poetry is somebody standing up, so to speak, and saying, with as little concealment as possible, what it is for him or her to be on earth at this moment."

Look at our New Testament. Christ's words are sanctified for their healing, nurturing, blessing, challenging, and gathering power, but he generally spoke in familiar terms and by analogy, for the Gospel of Matthew tells us, "he told the crowds all these things in parables; without parables he told them nothing."

"At its simplest," the Welsh theologian C. H. Dodd wrote, "the parable is a metaphor or simile drawn from nature or common life, arresting the hearer by its vividness or strangeness, and leaving the mind in sufficient doubt about its precise application to tease it into active thought."

Our Bible is an anthology of such stories, each having what may be a very personal meaning and one that can only be "teased out" or arrived at through interpretation or, better, meditation. In a similar manner, imaginative writing has the possibility of serving as a religious experience as the fiction writer, playwright, or poet uses invented lives and language to entertain, educate, and perhaps guide readers toward making correct moral and ethical choices.

Elsewhere I published an essay entitled "What Stories Are and Why We Read Them" in which I noted that:

> Stories teach by example, and by permitting us to safely participate in crises we hope to never get near. Quotidian life seldom offers opportunities for glorious heroism or grand agonies of defeat, but fictional entertainments offer those opportunities in abundance. . . Ethical grayness characterizes much of our human experience; and we change only incrementally, through a host of seemingly inconsequential decisions. The zest of good storytelling comes from its gross exaggeration of the frightening and mysterious process of change, so that we see heightened in *The English Patient* or *Schindler's List* the horrifying possibilities of wrong choices and the health to ourselves and others in choosing rightly.

Making things up, for me, is both extraordinarily simple and rather mysterious. I recognize first that I am gripped: a subject presents itself to me as one I need to deal with, a story I have to tell. One by one, fictional scenes occur to me like many stairsteps to an upper room. Seeing, hearing, and feeling the locale, the weather, and the characters enables me to become a participant in each scene and, no matter the topic, my own emotional, psychological, or spiritual concerns are highlighted or weeded out. I solve issues not in the random, chaotic way of dreaming but through orderly focus and conjecture.

A like experience happens as we read, for, whether we're aware of it or not, we're making things up just as the author is, putting faces on those who have not been described, filling in details left out, questioning what we would do in those circumstances, or recalling times when we were vexed in just that way.

I have visited some twelve- step meetings with friends and have been struck by the earthy, frank, hair-raising, and sometimes hilarious reminiscences of men and women who are coming to terms with their addiction. The confessions are ways of repenting for a history of excesses, establishing a new transparency, reforming one's own life by connecting it with others while disconnecting it from the past, and sharing in the sheer gift of recovery.

Hearing those acts of reconciliation has always reminded me of Garrison Keillor's insistence on "the obligation we all have to tell stories." We sit around a kitchen table or huddle over cups of coffee or queue up for a movie ticket, and as we confess or joke or prevaricate with each other, we may think we are just killing time, but we are forming a kind of church. There are grander things we can aspire to, magnificent projects we can take on, but it is the holiness of the ordinary that is, I think, what the writers of the twenty-first century are called to notice and seek out.

Jack London maintained, "I write for no other purpose than to add to the beauty that now belongs to me. I write a book for no other reason than to add three or four hundred acres to my magnificent estate."

We are better for having written well. We are better for reading. We are enlarged. And we are connected with something ancient.

On the first page of *Look Homeward, Angel*, Thomas Wolfe has it that:

> Each of us is all the sums he has not counted: subtract us into nakedness and night again, and you shall see begin in Crete four thousand years ago the love that ended yesterday in Texas. The seed of our destruction will blossom in the desert, the alexin of our cure grows by a mountain rock, and our lives are haunted by a Georgia slattern, because a London cutpurse went unhung. Each moment is the fruit of forty thousand years.

Each moment on earth, in fact, is the fruit of eons. Instinctively we all know that, but there are still times when we feel like discoverers of something momentous and feel the need to proclaim what has been hidden but now found. And so we all make things up. We describe what we have seen that took on an acute and sudden importance for us. We repeat something we have heard not just to get rid of it, but to revere whatever inhabited it that gave it permanence in our minds. We tell each other stories to remember, entertain, console, repent, inspire, and in a hundred other ways flesh out our roles in the great drama of civilization.

# SEEING INTO THE MIDDLE OF THINGS

LOOK AT FOUR QUOTATIONS FROM THE ESSAY "ATTENTION AND WILL" by the great French philosopher Simone Weil.

She wrote: "Attention, taken to its highest degree, is the same thing as prayer. It presupposes faith and love."

She wrote: "Extreme attention is what constitutes the creative faculty in us, and the only extreme attention is religious."

She wrote: "The attention turned with love towards God (or in a lesser degree, towards anything which is truly beautiful) makes certain things impossible for us. Such is the non-acting action of prayer in the soul."

She wrote: "The highest ecstasy is the attention at its fullest."

I hesitate to try to explain those quotations, for they seem to me to function as koans or parables that ought to be left alone to the stress of meditation. But I would like to at least linger a while in the proximity of Simone Weil's concept of attention, which she seems to describe both as seeing and as a form of expectant waiting.

***

I have taken as my title the definition for the Mayan word, *Nicuachinel*, meaning "shaman," or "he who sees into the middle of things." And it seems to me that is the gift or desire of most of us: to see into the middle of things.

I have taught a parish Bible study class on the Epistles of Saint Paul, so I have had the opportunity to read once again his gorgeously rhetorical encouragement to the Christians in Corinth, in which he wrote: "When I was a child, I spoke like a child, I understood like a child, I thought like a child: but when I became a man, I put away childish things. For now we see through a glass, darkly; but then we shall see face to face: now I know only in part; but then shall I know fully even as I have been fully known" (1 Cor 13:11–12).

To know fully, even as we have been fully known. A friend who is a psychotherapist once told me she thought the foremost reason that people marry was not loneliness or lust or security. Rather, they yearn to be fully known by a husband or wife and to share in the intimate gift of fully knowing another.

We seek a deep and perceptive insight into ourselves that we can only get through intimacy with another, and we read fictional narratives and memoirs for just that reason, too, "for now," as Saint Paul wrote, "we see through a glass, darkly." We have in front of us guises, personae, and outward appearances. We yearn for the *secret* life of our times. We yearn to "see face to face."

Wondering about that gerund "seeing," I researched the physiology of sight and found that only in the most limited way do our eyes function like cameras. Right behind the iris and pupil is a lens that focuses images, upside-down, onto the retina at the rear of the eye. There is the equivalent of an exposure setting at work so that we can note fine details in enough sunshine, and at night gradually adjust to the darkness and fuzzily recognize shapes, but not in color. Like cameras we can change the focal length of the lenses by squeezing or widening the internal optics. We have no shutters, of course. We do not lock onto an image. We scan it. Even when we presume we're staring and the image is fixed, we're actually shifting our focus ever so slightly so that varying measures of light will hit the retina and cause it to zap signals along the optic nerve into the brain, refreshing and updating the image at such great speed that we perceive our vision as seamless. When we speak of seeing we're speaking of the hard mental activity of decoding, for we *see* through pattern recognition. We collect nuanced notes about edges, shapes, colors, and motion, and we rather instantaneously work at interpreting them. And though we're not aware of it, that mental processing is so exhausting that scientists have estimated that close to 40 percent of our at-rest caloric consumption is devoted to the necessary interpretations of sight. The only job of a huge percentage of our higher brain function is recognizing what's right in front of us.

In *Pilgrim at Tinker Creek*, Annie Dillard noted the experiences of those Western surgeons who'd first performed cataract operations on the blind. Doctors found that patients who could recognize forms such as a cube or sphere with their hands or tongues and then name them could not relate that tactile information to what was held in front of them when they finally could see. A girl recorded the sensations all infants must have, of registering nothing but many patches of brightness. Another patient reported that he now saw only a field of light, "in which everything appeared dull, confused, and in motion."

Even distances were puzzling. Thomas Aquinas once stated that we are born with the faculty to recognize that the sun is not the size of an orange, but that seems not to have been the case. We each learn that skill as babies by seeking out and grabbing some things near at hand while failing to attain what is far away. Infants sometimes reach for the moon. The formerly blind grown-ups who'd been operated on in Annie Dillard's account found that the world which seemed so static and small when they were non-seeing was suddenly overwhelming in its chaos and size. Everything had seemed closer, their houses cozier, when they were blind.

We who've grown up seeing are used to it, but some post-operative grownups were now humiliatingly aware that they had been visible all this time and that their privacy had been invaded over the years by anyone who shot a glance in their direction. Some preferred to shut their eyes when in their homes in order to walk about in their old way. Doctors also noticed a loss of serenity and a change in habits as the newly sighted now groomed themselves, envied others, sought false and misleading appearances, even lied and stole.

But there were others who were stunned by the variety and richness of the world, one girl recording her astonishment that each person she looked at had a recognizably different face. Another expressing gratification and surprise as she saw so much for the first time and could only gasp, "Oh God! How beautiful!"

And yet we miss so much. As Annie Dillard points out, "I see within the range of only about 30 percent of the light that comes from the sun; the rest is infrared and some little ultraviolet, perfectly apparent to many animals, but invisible to me. A nightmare network of ganglia, charged and firing without my knowledge, cuts and splices what I do see, editing it for my brain."

Of such facts are science fictions made. I owned a cat named Skeezix that would stare with fascination at nothing at all, insofar as I could tell, but perhaps Skeezix was seeing some of that 70 percent of "whatever" that was unavailable to me. I have no idea what I'm missing in those colors I am unable to discern, but the quest to see ever more seems a characteristic human trait. We are predatory in that way. And as biologist Bruce Boff has pointed out, "Colors do not exist in the material world. Photons of different wavelengths do." An immaterial mind, or consciousness, or soul "converts whatever happens physically in the brain into our perceptions, including color."

We are limited, too, by time. Whether we realize it or not, we see anything for only the particle of an instant. Either the image is updated, or it's history, just a thing remembered. I find Kurt Vonnegut fascinating on this when he writes of the wider perspective of his deep space aliens, the Tralfamadorians, in *Slaughterhouse-Five*. The premise of that novel is that an optometrist who is aptly named Billy Pilgrim has become "unstuck in time." Billy can be in his backyard hammock in Ilium, New York in 1963, then find himself in World War II when he was a soldier imprisoned by the Nazis in a slaughterhouse during the Allied firebombing of Dresden, and then Billy can abruptly jump to the future and his zoological life with the luscious actress Montana Wildhack on the planet of Tralfamadore.

Writing about his timeless adventures to his local newspaper, Billy explains:

"All moments, past, present, and future, always have existed, always will exist. The Tralfamadorians can look at all the different moments just the way we can look at a stretch of the Rocky Mountains, for instance. They can see how permanent all the moments are, and they can look at any moment that interests them. It is just an illusion we have here on Earth that one moment follows another one, like beads on a string, and that once a moment is gone it is gone forever.'"

Recognizing that all our glimpses are fleeting, we hold onto some of them through mechanical means or through description. I hold up a favorite snapshot and as I contemplate it a forgotten memory is nudged forward, an emotion is churned up, I may even hear snatches of the music that was playing when someone with foresight took out her camera and said, "Smile."

In a journal entry by the nineteenth-century British Jesuit poet Gerard Manley Hopkins, he famously noted that "what you look hard at seems to look back at you."

Hopkins seems to have gotten that notion via the Oxford University art historian John Ruskin, whose handbook *The Elements of Drawing* was a bestseller in England when Hopkins was in high school and which inspired Gerard's enthusiasm for recording the natural world.

Just as nineteenth century science had acquired the habit of classifying, closely watching, and exactingly recording the attributes and activities of flora and fauna, so Ruskin urged those who would be educated to find the grand significance in even seemingly inconsequential and transitory realities.

Ruskin approached the theological in his belief that only an impartial and fearless seeing leads to "noble emotion" which in turn leads to a revelation of nature as God's work, his holy book. Ruskin held that "all great art is praise and that faithful observation of the facts of existence would result in fresh disclosures of the Holy Being for humanity."

Hopkins seems to have written no poetry that counted from 1867, when he graduated from Oxford University, to December 1875 when the tragic loss at sea of five nuns exiled from Germany inspired him to compose "The Wreck of the Deutschland." But in those eight years of elected silence, Hopkins was journaling about a natural world that he observed with reverence, just as Ruskin recommended.

This is from his journal of a vacation on the Isle of Man in August 1872: "Again to Port Soderick. This time it was a beautiful day. I looked down from the cliffs at the sea breaking on the rocks at high-water of a spring tide—first, say, it is an install of green marble knotted with ragged white, then fields of white lather, the comb of the wave richly clustered and crisped in breaking, then it is broken small and so unfolding till it runs in threads and thrums twitching down the backdraught to the sea again."

In another journal entry Hopkins notes that: "When the wave ran very high it would brim over on the sloping shelf below me and move smoothly and steadily along it like the palm of a hand along a table drawing off the dust." And he describes "one little square house cushioned up in a thatched grove of green like a man with an earache."

In his journals and in his poetry, Hopkins saw into the middle of things. Seeing gave rise to feeling and closely observed actualities gave rise to religious emotion, as in his famous hymn to creation, "Pied Beauty":

> Glory be to God for dappled things—
> For skies of couple-colour as a brinded cow;
> For rose-moles all in stipple upon trout that swim;
> Fresh-firecoal chestnut-falls; finches' wings;
> Landscape plotted and pieced—fold, fallow, and plough;
> And áll trádes, their gear and tackle and trim.
>
> All things counter, original, spare, strange;
> Whatever is fickle, freckled (who knows how?)
> With swift, slow; sweet, sour; adazzle, dim;
> He fathers-forth whose beauty is past change:
>     Praise him.

In variation, complexity, and juxtapositions Hopkins finds in the natural world declarations of the infinite extent of God's glorious, imaginative activity. Because of how Hopkins so acutely saw the world, God could seem very near and self-illuminating in the best of times, when even a falcon rocking and hovering over its prey could remind him of Christ, and in the weariness and desolation in which he wrote his so-called "terrible sonnets," Hopkins could find God remote and humanity loathsome, mere carrion, and in anguish write of himself, "I am gall, I am heartburn."

It was Hopkins who inspired the French Jesuit Pierre Teilhard de Chardin to develop a theology based on an examination of the "within" of things and to choose "information" as the word that most usefully describes the influence of Jesus Christ in the Cosmos.

"What you look hard at seems to look back at you." *Right* seeing is relational. Jewish philosopher Martin Buber would explore that idea in his classic *I and Thou*, in which he pictured a tree as a pillar with flowing green leaves in a flood of light, a species in "infinite commerce with earth and air."

Buber wrote, "Throughout all of this the tree remains my object and has its place and its time span, its kind and condition.

"But it can also happen, if will and grace are joined, that as I contemplate the tree I am drawn into relation, and the tree ceases to be an It. The power of exclusiveness has seized me . . .

"The tree is no impression, no play of my imagination, no aspect of a mood; it confronts me bodily and has to deal with me as I must deal with it—only differently.

"One should not try to dilute the meaning of the relation: relation is reciprocity," Martin Buber wrote.

Relation and reciprocity are features of all our contacts with the arts. We view or read or hear and our first step is generally acceptance, welcoming any presence of beauty, willing to be moved, hoping for the best, which is friendship with the piece. Our secondary impulse is evaluation. Early humans needed to conjure decisions on the basis of hunger and fear, to conjure if what they saw was food or a predator and if they should fight or flee. Our discriminations are calmer but no less affecting. There is still a vital presence of friend or foe in our encounter, but now we are judging whether it dangerously opposes our values and attitudes or is just something we can comfortably ignore. Walk away from. And the third step is often that of self-inquiry. Examination of conscience, if you will. Why did I react that way? Was I fair? How was I delighted or offended? What buttons did it push? Seeing—that is, intelligent sensing—is always transactional.

I have had the experience of picking up a book, reading a few pages, and loathing it. And then just a few years later, giving it another chance in which I find myself wondering just what it was I so disliked earlier. Each page now seems touched with genius. (We need to note, of course, that genius is frequently repellent at first because genius, by its nature, disrupts our expectations.)

And there is a corollary experience of recollecting a gorgeous passage in a book, hunting for it, and finding it isn't there: I have fantasized it. We are co-creators of the works of art we view or hear or read.

Reading the *Holy Sonnets* of John Donne, an Anglican priest who died in 1631, almost four hundred years ago, I page to sonnet number ten and the first lines "Death be not proud, though some have called thee / Mighty and dreadfull, for, thou art not so . . ." And because I know the poem well, I skirt ahead to the final couplet: "One short sleepe past, wee wake eternally, / And death shall be no more; death, thou shalt die."

Wow! can only communicate the explosion I feel with "death, thou shalt die," because the phrase has combined with what I know of London and Saint Paul's Cathedral, where John Donne was Dean, and with that there are my own remembrances of loved ones who have died, the first of them Christ, or those who have recovered from cancer, and then there is Margaret Edson's miracle of a play, Wit, in which the sonnet is featured and commented on, and then there's the glorious film adaptation of Wit by Emma Thompson and Mike Nichols, which I defy you to view without, in the end, weeping. The layering can go on and on, each recollection deepening and enriching the first glance at the poem.

Ingmar Bergman's film adaptation of Amadeus Mozart's The Magic Flute begins with an overture in which the camera simply roams over the faces of expectant people in an opera audience. We, as an audience ourselves, have no place to go, so we watch the faces as the overture plays, and we find in our attentiveness, in Ingmar Bergman's attentiveness, that all those faces are interesting. There are none that I recall fulfilling my own culture-enforced standards of beauty, but Mozart's music, their rapt expressions, and even the peculiarities and flaws of physiognomy united in a harmony, call it a chord, that included those of us in the movie theater seats, and I recall feeling a great happiness, a joy in community. And I realized I needed to look closer at the world. To be more attentive.

Simone Weil also wrote: "Those who are unhappy have no need for anything in this world but people capable of giving them their attention." She meant there was a holiness, whose expression was joy and sympathy and self-giving, for those who have not just focused on but related to a person, an object, or an idea.

We who feel we have been watched and loved and enjoyed by the Holy One have exactly that feeling of generosity and attention. Against all logic and sense of proportion, we each seem to matter. Culture and faith are united, in various ways, of saying just that.

Right after Adam and Eve eat the forbidden fruit of the tree of the knowledge of good and evil, "They heard the sound of the Lord God walking in the garden at the time of the evening breeze, and the man and his wife hid themselves." I have always been charmed by the notion of the Almighty ambling in the evening breeze, perhaps with a jaunty cane and a boater like Maurice Chevalier. But it's the hiding that is crucial to the passage. God calls out, "Where are you?" and Adam seemingly skulks from behind the scenery and into view, squeamishly replying, "I heard the sound of you in the garden and I was afraid because I was naked, and I hid myself."

In the sly, funny, insightful way of folk art, the birth of human self-consciousness is here displayed, and the fruitless efforts at escape from our all-seeing God is given its origin. At least Adam had the temerity to be truthful at first, but he almost immediately shirks from responsibility, coldly identifying Eve as "the woman whom you gave to be with me," and ratting her out as the initiator who gave him the fruit from the tree.

I find the rest of the fable, in which a wrathful God evicts Adam and Eve from paradise and condemns them to labor and pain, far less interesting than the first part of the story with its psychological reality that the Spirit of God is frequently calling out to us, "Where are you?" And it's still a human tendency to hide or avoid contact with God, to shirk our responsibilities, feel ashamed, claim no ownership of our sins, even to lie about them. We think that God only loves the prettiest aspects of ourselves and the good things that we do; that he congratulates us on our successes but would just as soon not see us as we are in our flawed humanity with all its ugliness, pettiness, weakness, and vulnerabilities.

There have been some psychological (and controversial) researchers who have found a strong linkage between creative genius and madness. But as Tom Bartlett wrote in *The Chronicle of Higher Education*, there are other researchers who have "a nicer, more democratic view, one that sees creativity as a capacity to be nurtured and developed, something all of us possess, perhaps to varying degrees, rather than a rarified ability tragically paired with affliction."

To overlook means both to view from on high, in panorama, and also to forgive or ignore indulgently. The gift of the arts, whether narrative or representative, is that they *overlook* our lives just as God does, giving us a sane, stabilizing sense of overview and even perhaps welcome or at least generous attention to our elations, our fears, our sins, our yearnings, and our plights. The gift of fiction, poetry, memoir, and all the arts is to let us see others in their most unprotected moments, the moments in which they are fallow ground, and then see them cultivated, or not, under our watchful and caring eyes.

Thomas Hardy famously noted that "The business of the poet and the novelist is to show the sorriness underlying the grandest things and the grandeur underlying the sorriest things."

Although Hardy limited his comment to creative writing, his thought on seeing into the middle of things is also the joy and obligation for all of us who consider ourselves attuned to the various signatures of God in the world.

The religious nature of this seeing is illustrated in Mary Oliver's wonderful poem "The Summer Day." She begins with the first line "Who made the world?" Then she notices a grasshopper that "has flung herself out of the grass" to eat sugar the poet holds in her hand. After fully describing the grasshopper and watching it fly away, she shifts from acute observation to mystical insight:

> I don't know exactly what a prayer is.
> I do know how to pay attention, how to fall down
> into the grass, how to kneel down in the grass,
> how to be idle and blessed, how to stroll through the fields,
> which is what I have been doing all day.
> Tell me, what else should I have done?
> Doesn't everything die at last, and too soon?
> Tell me, what is it you plan to do
> with your one wild and precious life?

The prophet Malachi wrote of the LORD: "But who can endure the day of His coming? And who shall stand when He appears? For He is like a refiner's fire, and like fuller's soap" (Mal 3:2).

You possibly already know that fuller's soap was used in Palestine to get wool its absolute whitest before it was sewn into clothing. Refiner's fire referred to the purification in the production of silver, which obligated the silversmith to watch the furnace for a good length of time without fail, for if the refining was exceeded for just a few seconds, the silver would be corrupted. And the typical way for a silversmith to recognize when the process of purification was complete was when he could *see his own reflection in the silver.*

The Spirit of God is working even now to see its own reflection in the Church, in the joys and sorrows of our being, in all of our quotidian lives. Our continuing goal ought to be that we become truth-tellers and truth-seekers: to attend to and confront the world honestly, unblinkingly, celebrating the beauty of creation, but not shying from its confusions, distortions, and sin. We need to permit the songs of innocence and experience an equal place in the hymnal. Without squeamishness or defensiveness or false piety and reserve.

And I return to Simone Weil, who wrote: "Attention, taken to its highest degree, is the same thing as prayer." Who wrote: "Extreme attention is what constitutes the creative faculty in us, and the only extreme attention is religious." Who wrote: "The attention turned with love towards God makes certain things impossible for us. Such is the non-acting action of prayer in the soul."

# ON THE GOSPEL ACCORDING TO MARK

We have no certainty about the author of *The Gospel accord-ing to Mark*. The epistles of Paul mention a Mark who was a co-worker and the cousin of Barnabas, but Mark or Marcus was a common name then. In *The Acts of the Apostles* there are mentions of a John Mark who was the son of a Jewish-Christian woman in Jerusalem, but his presumed gospel seems to find Judaism a foreign religion and his description of the geography of Palestine is frequently faulty so there's cause for doubt. Hippolytus of Rome maintained that Mark the evangelist, Mark the cousin of Barnabas, and the John Mark who accompanied Paul in *The Acts of the Apostles* were the same man, one of the seventy disciples sent out by Jesus to proselytize. But Eusebius of Caesarea linked him to the apostle Peter as a companion and interpreter among the Greeks. Peter's sermons, Eusebius claimed, be-came the basis for this gospel. It was said that a Mark founded and became bishop of the Church of Alexandria in 49 CE and the Coptic tradition states that he was martyred in 68. Yet, there is still no firm linkage to the gospel we have before us. Even the attribution "According to Mark" was not on the oldest gospel text we have.

I imagine him as a serious, enthusiastic, extroverted young man, even initially an adolescent, who first heard the compelling stories of Pe-ter about his Lord Jesus in some Greek locale, became a devoted disciple, and followed the apostle to Rome, where he also met Paul. He was wowed by both of them. There is so much that is headlong, hurried, panting, and overtly passionate in his narrative that it is impossible to think it the considered product of an older man or woman. Note how often he uses the words "Suddenly" or "Immediately." The speed of development in his gospel bespeaks the vitality and impatience of youth.

I imagine him accumulating the facts of the life of Jesus that Peter and Paul were sure of and collecting them in a narrative that he could speak aloud to listeners in whichever *ecclesia* he visited, probably those in and around Rome, and counting on his conviction, earnestness, and fervor to conquer any skepticism from his listeners.

Characteristic of his good news is an amazing vividness of detail, as in the description of the insanity and convulsive struggles of the Gerasene demoniac. Compare Mark 5:1–20 with the scene in Matthew 8:28—9:1, where there are two madmen drunk with evil who "were so fierce that no one could pass that way." That's as full as the description gets.

Whereas in Mark we hear of just one man with an unclean spirit whose fierceness is given particularity and the immediacy of drama. "He had often been restrained with shackles and chains, but the chains he wrenched apart, and the shackles he broke in pieces; and no one had the strength to subdue him. Night and day among the tombs and on the mountains he was always howling and bruising himself with stones" (5:3–5).

Look at Luke 8:43–48 concerning the "woman who had been suffering from hemorrhages for twelve years." There are many similarities to Mark's portrayal in 5:25–34, but Luke "The Physician" considers the bleeding woman in a far more aloof, objective way and summarizes that "though she had spent all she had on physicians, no one could cure her."

Whereas Mark sympathizes with her frustration with medicine in noting "she was no better, but rather grew worse"(5:26). Mark also gives the scene greater intimacy by entering the mind of the afflicted woman and permitting her to state her intention: "She had heard about Jesus, and came up behind him in the crowd and touched his cloak, for she said, 'If I but touch his cloak, I will be made well'" (5:27–28).

In his treatment of Jesus himself, Mark indicates emotions and interiority that are often missing from the other gospel accounts. Jesus meets a leper and is "moved with pity" (1:41). When he warns the cured leper not to speak of his healing to the priests, he does so "sternly" (1:43). In 6:6 Jesus is rejected by his former friends and neighbors in Nazareth and is "amazed at their unbelief." Questioned by Pharisees in 8:11, Jesus's exasperation is telegraphed by Mark saying, "he sighed deeply in his spirit." And when he is asked by the rich man what he must do to inherit eternal life, "Jesus, looking at him, loved him" (10:21).

Seemingly like Mark himself, Jesus is in a hurry, an urgency communicated by rapid shifts in scenes and continuing use of "and" as if only the conventions of grammar kept him from writing his gospel in one long sentence.

It's only as Mark nears the account of Jesus's Passion that the pace slows down. His final day of betrayal, trials, and crucifixion is even given novelistic suspense by a conscientious notation of the hour when various events occurred. In meditating on this gospel, I once found myself dreaming that Jesus and I were on the banks of a brook. Jesus told me he had to cross it and enter Holy Week, for "I *am* my death." I haven't yet solved the meaning of that announcement, but it seems a sentiment shared by Mark.

Another way in which he increases suspense can be seen in chapter 6. Jesus orders the Twelve to go out among the villages, tell the good news, cast out demons, and heal the sick (6:7–13). However, Mark interrupts that account with the famous story of Herod's beheading of John the Baptist in 6:14–29, only to go back to the apostles who have returned from the villages and report "all that they had done and taught" (6:30). In biblical scholarship it's called "the Markan sandwich"; in film it's called "cross-cutting." We see an activity, jump to another locale, and learn what's happening simultaneously, then go back to the original event, either to contrast the separate narratives or to interpret them. In this case, Mark is foreshadowing the beheadings and crucifixions that would be visited on most of the persecuted apostles within forty years.

Because this gospel seems to have been initially an oral narrative, Mark needed to repeat crucial words and phrases for the comprehension of his listening audience, to give them common purchase by echoing familiar Old Testament texts, to hint at future occurrences while also reminding them of things past, and to provide "asides" that educate a Gentile population about customs, geography, and vocabulary that would have been foreign to them. Essentially, he is a good teacher who simply and compellingly guides his students to his core proclamation: that there once was a man among them who was also the Son of God, and he was crucified but rose from the dead as a sign of the salvation that he promised all who had faith in him.

As a fiction writer, I'm overwhelmed by the stunning artistry of this gospel, in the interweavings of his tapestry, with no thread frazzled or forgotten, no scene without vibrant color or meaning. Everything in this gospel is necessary, and as with the finest poetry one can find something new with each reading.

I once worked in a parish's pre-catechumenate where we coaxed those who were making their first hesitant steps toward entrance into the Church, often with no religious training in their background. I made the suggestion to one middle-aged man that he experience the gospel just as villagers did when the evangelist we call Mark proclaimed it: that he read the whole narrative in one sitting—it's just thirty-five pages long in the Bible I use. I did not see that man again until one weekday Mass when the newly-minted Catholic rushed over to shake my hand and thank me for that introduction to Christianity. He was, as we say, blown away—not just by Mark's powerful storytelling nor his wondrous assertions about Christ, but by the limerence he felt for Jesus and the way that emotion seemed reciprocated by genuine, holy, everlasting love. Such is the grace available to all who read this great gospel.

# SPIRITUAL EXERCISES

IÑIGO DE LOYOLA WAS A DEVIL-MAY-CARE, TWENTY-SIX-YEAR-OLD squire to the King of Castile when his leg was shattered in the battle of Pamplona. In his long convalescence in the family manor, Iñigo underwent a religious conversion that inspired him to give up his former ways and live a penitential hermit's life in Manresa, Spain, on the banks of the river Cardoner. With the guidance of a Benedictine spiritual director, and under the influence of books such as *The Imitation of Christ* by Thomas à Kempis and the *Vita Christi* of Ludolph of Saxony, Iñigo penned in incorrect Spanish a notebook record of the consolations, graces, and inner wrenchings he experienced while meditating on scripture, and through which God kindly educated him "as the schoolmaster does a child."

The crucial insight Iñigo had was that his Manresa notebook could become a practical manual in escorting others through mystical contact with their soul's deepest yearnings and thus with God. Calling the journal *Spiritual Exercises*, and jotting additions to it as he went along, Iñigo carried it with him on his journey north to the University of Paris in 1528. He was thirty-seven years old, with little money, and could only communicate with the international population of the Sorbonne with a sketchy Latin. But one by one the scrawny, limping, charismatic mendicant persuaded his much younger classmates to retreat from the world with his exercises for a month, and one by one they became his "friends in the Lord" until seven of them professed the vows that were the first step to forming the Society of Jesus.

Iñigo López de Loyola was by then a Master of Arts and was calling himself Ignatius. In three years he would be ordained a priest and soon after that become the Superior General of a congregation headquartered in Rome and officially approved by Pope Paul III. But Ignatius never ceased giving his Spiritual Exercises and consented to have his finer Latin translation of them published in 1548.

Ignatius wrote that his Spiritual Exercises "have as their purpose the conquest of self and the regulation of one's life in such a way that no decision is made under the influence of any inordinate attachment." The first week of the exercises requires a scrupulous examination of our life history, seeing God's loyal and loving presence within it, but also acknowledging the sins, addictions, and predilections that hindered our possibilities. The first week ends with a meditation on Christ's call for us to follow him, with the promise that we will lead richer, happier lives.

The second week essentially teaches us how to follow Christ more closely by establishing us as his disciples. We watch his birth and accompany him in his baptism in the river Jordan, his sermon on the mount, his raising of Lazarus from the dead, and other healing and teaching events in his public ministry. Empowered by the love of God and our friendship with Jesus, we are required to make a choice of a way of life, a choice that may involve a great change in our habits or careers, but more often entails only those amendments and reformations that enhance a closer relationship with God.

Intimacy with Jesus having been established, we witness in the third week his last supper, the agony in the garden, his arrest and trials, and his passion and death. The fourth week is devoted to Jesus's resurrection and his various apparitions to his disciples, concluding with a "Contemplation to Attain the Love of God."

The method for each hour's meditation is generally the same. We begin with a preparatory prayer and as a prelude to the meditation consider the history of the subject, such as Jesus appearing to seven of his disciples as they fished on the Sea of Galilee (John 21:1–17), reading the gospel passage several times until we can develop a mental representation of the locale and the people in it. We then ask for a grace; in this case, it is to be consoled at seeing Christ on the shore and to feel the joy and comfort of his resurrection. We see the fishermen hauling in their nets, hear the smack of waves against the boat's hull, feel the sunshine on our skins, smell seaweed and flotsam, taste the water we scoop up in our palm. With all five senses wholly engaged, we become part of the scene and can be as shocked and happy as Peter was when he recognized that it was the risen Christ who was roasting a fish on a charcoal fire on the shore and plunged into the sea to wade to him. We hear Christ's instruction to Peter, and we also enter the conversation—or as Ignatius puts it, colloquy—inquiring, perhaps, on how we ourselves can feed his sheep or simply saying, like Peter, "Lord, you know that I love you." We finish the meditation period with a standard prayer, such as the Our Father, and usually exercitants keep a journal in which they describe what happened in their prayer and its effect on them.

Ignatius found early on that there were those who were "educated or talented but engaged in public affairs or necessary business" who could not find a free month to perform the exercises as he'd first intended. For them he developed a program in which the Spiritual Exercises could be completed without withdrawal from jobs or other obligations by having the multiple exercises of the thirty days carried out in the course of thirty weeks—an increasingly popular choice for lay people. One of the greatest gifts of this so-called "19th annotation retreat" is that it teaches a habit of prayer that can be incorporated throughout our lives—that journey with God that Ignatius called "the fifth week."

# A JOURNEY IN THE LAND CALLED HOLY

THE JESUS MOVIES FROM THE FIFTIES AND SIXTIES PREPARED ME FOR A different landscape. I expected Israel to be flatlands and sand, the kind of sunburnt hardscrabble you find in West Texas. But on the bus ride north from the international airport in Tel Aviv, I found rolling hills of wheat and sorghum, lush green grass, wild yellow mustard and broom plants, and large fist-like boulders of limestone, sandstone, and chalk that seemed to grow out of the earth like a crop.

I was with a hundred fortunate travelers on a week-long tour of the Holy Land based on *Jesus: A Pilgrimage* by James Martin, SJ, our host. Our initial lodging was in an Italian Franciscan hotel that was called Mount of the Beatitudes because of its location on the steep hillside where Jesus delivered his famous contrarian sermon.

About a half hour before Sunday's dawn, while a rooster crowed in the yard of the hotel, the jet-lagged members of our party waited in the half-dark on a promenade two hundred feet above a hazy gray Sea of Galilee. The trees were filled with the lovely noise of waking, chirping finches and larks, swallows and warblers until a golden sun seemed to gradually ignite over the hills of the azure Golan Heights and then serenely moved overhead. We all had to have been stunned by the same bracing thought: *Jesus woke to this.*

The Sea of Galilee was larger than I had imagined. It is thirteen miles long, eight miles at its greatest width and, at 686 feet *below* sea level, the lowest freshwater lake in the world. Called Lake Gennesaret by the evangelist Luke and the Sea of Tiberias by John, the whole of it was formed by a volcano that temporarily dammed the flow of a Jordan river fed by springs and creeks in northern Lebanon. Rabbis wrote of it, "Although God has created seven seas, yet He has chosen this one as his special delight." Yet it can be violent, too, when the winds funnel down into the basin from the north. Waves as high as ten feet have been recorded surging over the downtown streets of Tiberias.

The fishing is still good there on the lake: a kind of tilapia, or St. Peter's Fish, that is often cooked in a frying pan and served with the head, fins, and tail still on; a larger whiskered species of carp; and schools of the Kinneret sardines that were famously pickled in Magdala in New Testament times.

Our first day trip was north just a few miles to Capernaum, Jesus's hometown during his public ministry, and the harbored fishing village of Peter, Andrew, James, and John. The Roman centurion whose servant Jesus healed from afar is credited with the construction of the first century synagogue there, now in stately ruins. And recent excavations have discovered a warren of apartments with shared walls of square black basalt blocks, each "house" so small I was reminded of Mark Twain's complaint of his shipboard stateroom, that it was large enough to swing a cat in but not without damage to the cat. The church in Capernaum is high off the ground to reveal beneath its glass floor the stacked brown rock of a multi-room house reputed to be that of St. Peter, his wife, and the ill mother-in-law whose hot fever Jesus cooled with his touch.

Less than two miles south along the lakeshore was the shady glen of Tabgha—meaning in Greek "seven springs"—the site of Jesus's miraculous multiplication of loaves and fish for the thousands hungrily following him. And it was also the location of Christ's post-resurrection appearance to his fishermen disciples when, after eating the tilapia he'd cooked for them, he took Simon aside and told him "Thou art Peter, and upon this rock I will build my church, and the gates of Hell shall not prevail against it." An alternate name for the site, therefore, is Peter's Primacy because of the preeminence given him there.

The Sea of Galilee is at least twenty feet shallower now than it was in olden times, so giant boulders that waves must have burst against are now isolated on a swath of sand that we walked, some of us wading in the cool, clean, tranquil water. Each site we visited was introduced by a reading of a relevant passage from the Gospels and then there was an hour or so for contemplative prayer.

Writing in the 16th century, Ignatius asked those doing his Spiritual Exercises to apply all five senses to each biblical scene to give it tangible immediacy. It was a practice easily accomplished on a tour that was so like a graced retreat that I sometimes worried about breaking the silence.

Looking southwest from the Mount of the Beatitudes, one could see a rift in the green mountains, once forested with fir trees, where the 20-mile highway to Nazareth is now. But that road was a late invention. Jesus would have avoided the steep hills and dales in his hard trek from Nazareth to Capernaum by hiking northeast along a high ridgeline, with only a forced, jarring slide down a cliff to get to the fertile flatlands and the Sea.

We went to Nazareth on Monday, finding a busy, Palestinian, majority-Muslim city where there had been just a forgettable Jewish village when Jesus grew up there in a cave on a high hillside. We had Mass in the Basilica of the Annunciation in honor of the girl Mary's agreement, perhaps at age fourteen, to become a handmaid of the Lord and the mother of God's son. A few miles from Nazareth is Cana where Jesus performed his first miracle, or sign, by turning huge jars of water into wine at his mother's request. Married couples on our pilgrimage repeated their wedding vows in Cana, as did those committed to religious life.

In Magdala we lunched in a fine restaurant, then went out onto the Sea in excursion boats, drifting in hymns and a feeling of companionship with Jesus before visiting a museum dedicated to a newly recovered sailboat from the 1st century. Constructed with cedar planks and a variety of scrap wood, it was large enough to hold fifteen fishermen and flat-bottomed so that it could get close to the shoals to dragnet sardines. The sloops and yawls of my imagination were given a healthy adjustment.

Israel is just a sliver of a nation—half of it desert—that could fit tidily inside our Lake Michigan, so it was just a short journey south to get to Jericho in an oasis on the Wadi Qelt more than 800 feet below sea level. East of Jericho is felt to be the spot on the Jordan River where, in a gesture of humility, Jesus was baptized by an Elijah-like John. Father Martin accurately described the surprisingly narrow river's green as the color of Mountain Dew but it seemed to me more like a lawn pesticide. Still, some Russian Orthodox women with flimsy white linen sheets over their underwear risked repeated plunges into the Jordan in a renewal of their own baptisms.

The biblical Bethany is where Jesus dined with the sisters Martha and Mary and wept at the tomb of Lazarus before raising his dear friend to life. Established on the eastern slope of the Mount of Olives, Bethany was just a mile and a half from Jerusalem overland by foot but a longer circular ascent in our touring buses as they groaned in their climb to the high altitude of Jerusalem.

The Old City of Jerusalem is predominantly one or two-story white buildings on terraced heights that were furrowed by ravines and surrounded by a tall fortification of stone walls whose color the fancy would call ecru. Ringing the Old City are chains of high hills with fanciful names like Mount Scopus, Mount of Offence, and Mount of Evil Counsel.

We were staying outside the walls near the New Gate at the first-class Hotel Notre Dame that is run by a pontifical institute and is just a ten-minute walk to the Church of the Holy Sepulcher. But the first site we visited on Thursday was six miles south and biblically chronological: the birthplace of Jesus in Bethlehem (meaning "House of Bread"). The main entrance to the Church of the Nativity has become over many centuries of amendments such a small doorway that guests have to get on their hands and knees to crawl inside, and within is not a manger and the representative statuary of a tableau but the silver lamps and candles and jewels of Byzantine decoration. But Luke's gospel narrative which we heard at Mass still has an unmatched evocative power as it focuses both on the Christ-child in the manger and foreshadows his offering of himself as food at the Last Supper.

Late that afternoon some of us went into the Old City to pray at the so-called Wailing Wall, the lone hundred-yard long remains of the huge, grand Jewish temple built by Herod the Great on thirty-five acres. As I nodded in my own Kaddish, to my right was an angry old man in foul rags and tatters reading from a worn and much-used prayer book and to my left was a Hasid in a fine black suit and flat-brimmed hat who loudly recited Hebrew as he rocked in his lamentations and periodically twirled his hand overhead in histrionics I couldn't decipher. Yet I found myself admiring the intensity in both men and felt, *You are standing on holy ground.*

That holiness became more intense the next day as we celebrated Mass in a basilica at Gethsemane—Aramaic for "olive press"—and spent an hour in the adjacent garden of betrayal at the foot of the Mount of Olives. Jesus and the Twelve must have often withdrawn there because of the magical panorama of the deep Kidron Valley before them and its nearly vertical uphill rise to the high fortification around a city of Jerusalem that probably glinted gold with torchlight. But circumstances forced us then to imagine the Lord's final agony in the garden. Some of us sat pensively against the twisted olive trees, all too aware that we often have been sleeping disciples rather than sharers in the wracked nightwatch of Jesus. My thought was of what he wanted from me and I heard him say, *Your prayers and attention.* And the attention, it was clear, was not just to him; it was attention to the world.

The Lenten feeling became even more intense in the house of Caiaphas where Jesus was harnessed by ropes in order to be lowered through a cistern to a foul, infested pit where he spent the night, shackled, defeated, and utterly alone while his disciple Peter heated his hands by a fire and, as a rooster crowed, shamefully and fearfully denied he even knew the Nazarene. I found myself praying backward in time to give Jesus endurance, freedom from pain, and the solace of a final triumph over the unjust punishment and execution that was forthcoming.

The final Saturday on our pilgrimage began with a Via Dolorosa that began at Antonia, the praetorium where Pontius Pilate interrogated Jesus, and zig-zagged along alleyways between souvenir shops on a gentle rise of limestone pavement to Golgotha, or the "hill of the skull," which is now solely commemorated in a lavishly ornamented choir loft in the Church of the Holy Sepulcher. On the floor nearby is the flat, polished slab where the lifeless body of Jesus was laid out and anointed with myrrh and olive oil that had been provided by a wealthy follower, Joseph of Arimathea. He offered his own nearby limestone shelf, hewn from the wall of a cave, as interment for Jesus, and over the centuries it has become the holiest of shrines, one that you have to stoop to get inside, as was reported in the gospel accounts, and whose emptiness is further evidence of Christ's resurrection from the dead, the wonderful cause of our worship and pilgrimage.

We celebrated an Easter Mass before noon and that sunny afternoon visited the healing pool at Bethesda, which the Fourth Gospel described in a way that seemed allegorical but which recent excavations have revealed to be accurate. Right next to it is a pretty French church dedicated to St. Anne who is thought to have given birth to Mary the mother of God at that place. Our Palestinian guide Maheer sang a haunting Aramaic salute to Mary there and it felt like a poignant envoi sending us back to America with feelings of awe and enrichment and of having solved the mystery of a homeland filled with sacred energy that we want to return to soon.

I'll never again read the Gospels in the same way.

# A FRIENDSHIP BASED ON POETRY
## Hopkins & Bridges

THEY MET AT OXFORD UNIVERSITY IN 1863. QUEEN VICTORIA WAS forty-four and in the twenty-sixth year of her sixty-four year reign. Lord Palmerston was prime minister. London had just opened the world's first underground railway, running from Paddington to Farringdon Street. Royal Albert Hall was built. Otto von Bismarck was prime minister of Prussia. The American Civil War was in its second year. British explorers Speke and Grant established that the source of the Nile was in Uganda and named it Lake Victoria. Cultured people all drew and played a musical instrument and spent a good deal of time peering at rock formations or gazing at the sky, and many journal entries concerned dramatic armadas of clouds.

Charles Dickens was between the novels *Great Expectations* and *Our Mutual Friend*. Alfred Lord Tennyson, Britain's poet laureate, was at the height of his popularity following his *Idylls of the King*. Christina Rosetti had just published *Goblin Market and other poems*. Elizabeth Gaskell was establishing a reputation as a novelist with *Sylvia's Lovers*. Victor Hugo's novel *Les Misérables* was an international best seller. Another best seller in England was *The Elements of Drawing* by John Ruskin, a book that would greatly influence ways of seeing nature and weather for an entire generation of artists and readers.

Gerard Manley Hopkins entered Oxford University and his residential college of Balliol in April, 1863 for the eight-week Trinity term. Hopkins was eighteen, very smart, the oldest of eight children, and from the upper-middle class, his father Manley owning a firm of marine insurance adjusters. Manley was also a poet and the self-taught author of practical manuals, one ho-hum novel, a history of Hawaii, and was Hawaii's Consul-General in Great Britain—especially impressive achievements for a man who quit school at the age of fifteen.

Gerard himself was ginger-haired, perpetually pleasant, highly self-disciplined, and reportedly effeminate in his manner—he was aware of the irony of his middle name and generally did not use it. He was five-foot-three and so slight that his head seemed too large for his weedy frame, but although he would later often be characterized as ill and frail—his nickname in high school was "Skin"—he seems to have been healthy as a young man, for he swam in the cold ocean, regularly took twenty-five mile hikes, and he would climb to the highest limbs of a tree with the ease of someone scaling a ladder. A high school classmate later wrote of Hopkins that he had been "the nicest boy" at Highgate School: "Tenacious when duty was concerned, he was full of fun, rippling over with jokes, and chaff, facile with pencil and pen, with rhyming jibe or cartoon; good for his size at games and taking his part, but not as we did placing them first."

Robert Seymour Bridges went up to Corpus Christi College from Eton six months later for the fall, or Michaelmas, term. He was one month shy of his nineteenth birthday. His father had died when Robert was just a boy, and though Robert was the eighth of nine children, there was still enough of an inheritance that a job and a livelihood were never nettlesome questions for him, and for much of his life he was a gentleman of leisure. His fine features were called patrician, and he was considered so stunningly handsome that there were Oxford classmates who could not take their eyes off him and thought him "the possessor of the most beautiful face ever seen in a man." Sixty years later, his obituary in the London *Times* still spoke of his "great stature and fine proportions, his leonine head, deep eyes, expressive lips, and a full-toned voice, made more effective by a slight, occasional hesitation in his speech." He was over six feet tall and wide-shouldered, a man's man who played football and cricket and was the star oarsman for his college rowing team. And if he was cold, secretive, aggressively intolerant, and given, as an associate later wrote, to "petulant exhibitions of rudeness," he was also generous, romantic, softhearted, considerate, and was fond of "friendship, good wine, and mirth."

In many ways, Hopkins and Bridges were opposites, but in just as many ways they were destined to be friends. They were both beautifully educated intellectuals studying classical languages, both endorsed the aesthetic principles of the Oxford professors John Ruskin and Walter Pater, both deeply admired Pre-Raphaelite art, Elizabethan poetry, William Shakespeare, John Milton, and the seventeenth-century English composer Henry Purcell; and they generally deplored the same things. Hopkins was a good enough artist to have made it his profession, as two of his younger brothers did, and was particularly adept at sketching nature scenes. Bridges was highly musical, playing piano and violin, and he would later compose songs for the *Yattendon Hymnal* that are standards in the liturgies of the Church of England even now. Hopkins combined academic excellence and a sharp, penetrating mind with a love of mischief and puns. Bridges was gifted in the natural sciences, articulate in his criticisms, interestingly opinionated, and was, as one classmate later wrote, "delightfully grumpy."

Bridges's step-father was Reverend Doctor John Molesworth, an esteemed and wealthy Anglican clergyman, and since the age of ten Bridges's home had been the vicarage at Rochdale in Lancashire. Two of his older sisters would marry clergymen, another sister joined an Anglican priory of the Sisters of Mercy, and at Eton Bridges was a High Church boy who entertained the idea of priestly ordination. But Bridges and his step-father were hardly close—Robert's scant mentions of him in his letters are generally sarcastic—and by the time he went to Oxford his religious practice was social and formulaic; he fulfilled the churchly requirements of an English gentleman, but by the time he graduated he was an agnostic and in his sixties would look back on his earlier "ecclesiastical attractions" as ludicrous. Winston Churchill once said of himself, "I could hardly be called a pillar of the Church, I am more in the nature of a buttress, for I support it from the outside." Bridges would likely not have disassociated himself from that rather complacent aphorism.

He was a child of a century in which many writers, artists, and intellectuals not only abandoned Christianity but belief in God altogether. Charles Darwin's *On the Origin of Species by Means of Natural Selection* was published in 1859 and widened the rupture between science and faith that was initiated with the period of the Enlightenment. British philosopher

David Hume's eighteenth-century studies had urbanely dispensed with explanations of God as handed down by theologians. Edward Gibbon's *History of the Decline and Fall of the Roman Empire* pitilessly criticized Christianity's record of superstition, wickedness, and folly. And there were John Stuart Mill, Georg Wilhelm Friedrich Hegel, Thomas Carlyle, Karl Marx, and many other seminal thinkers whose antipathies were generating a cultural shift away from organized religion. A. N. Wilson has pointed out, in his intellectual history, *God's Funeral*, that by 1900, most British intellectuals had discarded the Christianity they grew up in.

With Hopkins, Christianity was still central. At Highgate School he'd ignored the ridicule of his classmates in order to keep a promise to his mother to read chapters of the New Testament each day. As an Oxford freshman he became involved in the High Church group organized by Reverend Henry Liddon, who sought to institute solemn liturgical ritual in Anglican services and to oppose the rationalism and theological liberalism that was emigrating from Germany by, as he put it, "reasserting and insisting upon the whole area of the Catholic Faith." Each Sunday night Hopkins attended Reverend Liddon's "Tea, Toast, and Testament" lectures in St. Edmund Hall, where he probably first met Bridges, and he began recording his sins and scruples in a confessional journal, a habit not unlike the nightly examination of conscience he would later practice as a Jesuit.

Writing to a friend, Hopkins indicated that he felt Roman Catholicism paradoxically intensified and subjectively destroyed what he called "the sordidness of things," and he felt that would be enough inducement to lead many people to the Roman Catholic Church. The legitimacy of Anglican dogma and sacraments, particularly that of High Communion, became a worry to him, the Sunday sermons he heard filled him with contempt, he thought of religious asceticism and even eternal punishment as ways of correcting "the triviality of this life." He read *Apologia Pro Vita Sua*, John Henry Newman's autobiographical account of his own religious conversion to the Church of Rome, and felt he'd found a kindred spirit. A friend noted in his journal entry of July 24th, 1866: "Walked out with Hopkins and he confided to me his fixed intention of going over to Rome. I did not attempt to argue with him as his grounds did not admit of argument."

Within a few weeks Hopkins was writing a letter to the Oxford alumnus Reverend Doctor John Henry Newman at his Oratory in Birmingham, saying he was anxious to become a Roman Catholic. "I do not want to be helped to any conclusions of belief," he wrote, "for I am thankful to say my mind is made up, but the necessity of becoming a Catholic... coming upon me suddenly has put me into painful confusion of mind about my immediate duty in my circumstances."

Bridges had invited Hopkins for a three-week vacation at the Rochdale vicarage before the fall term of 1866, and Hopkins hoped to confer with Reverend Newman about his conversion on his way there. But no reply to his letter immediately came, so Hopkins journeyed to Reverend and Mrs. Molesworth's home in a state of tension, impatience, and secrecy. Bridges and Hopkins hiked and lounged about, studied the intricacies of Greek grammar together, and spoke about poetry and music, but Hopkins was silent about the matter that was uppermost in his mind for he knew that Reverend and Mrs. Molesworth would view his conversion with a mixture of sorrow and alarm. And yet his taciturnity so troubled Bridges that Hopkins finally confessed his decision and was grateful that Bridges forgot his repugnance for what he would call "Romanism" in order to console his friend, even excusing Hopkins with the admission that his own "plain blurting disposition" would have been a daunting obstacle to anyone sharing his religious convictions. But in his suave condolence for his friend's emotional stress what Bridges was mainly demonstrating was his own indifference to religion.

Hopkins was accepted into the Roman Catholic Church by Reverend Newman on Sunday, October 21st, 1866. Expatriation might have been received with greater equanimity. Hearing the news, Manley Hopkins sorrowfully wrote his son, "O Gerard my darling boy are you indeed gone from me?" Reverend Edward Pusey, a professor of divinity at Oxford, nastily wrote his student that he was a "pervert"; and in a letter to Florence Nightingale, Benjamin Jowett, Hopkins's tutor, referred to him as one of "three foolish fellows at our College . . . [who] have gone over to Rome."

Bridges was not similarly estranged: he again invited Hopkins to Rochdale—Hopkins demurred—and just before Bridges sailed for a tour of Egypt and Syria, he stopped by the Hopkins's family home in Hampstead, hoping to find his friend there. And it was to Bridges that Hopkins first confided that on his Easter retreat he would try to decide if he had "a vocation to the priesthood." In 1868, even as he was heading to the novitiate of the Society of Jesus in southwest London, Hopkins stressed that there would be no impediment to their continued communications.

But there were. Bridges enrolled as a student at Saint Bartholomew's Hospital medical school in London in November, 1869, and his professional studies so occupied him that he seems to have visited his friend in the novitiate only once. And then either Bridges's profound distrust of the Jesuits, which was shared by much of Britain, or Hopkins's pedantic tendency to patronize on matters of faith and morals must have incited a chill in their friendship, for there is a gap of a year and a half in which we have no correspondence between them. At last, in 1871, when Hopkins had taken his first vows and gone up to Stonyhurst in Lancashire to study philosophy, he wrote "Dearest Bridges" apologetically: "I hear nothing whatever of you and the fault is certainly mine. I am going to address this to Rochdale, because you may have changed your lodgings in town . . . I shall not write more now, indeed I have nothing to say. Please tell me all about yourself. I am sure I must have behaved unkindly when you came to Roehampton."

Another gulf opened between them when Hopkins wrote his friend what he later jokingly referred to as his "red letter," in which he mentioned the political agitation in Europe, the squalor of Britain's cities, the miseries of the poor, and admitted that "Horrible to say, in a manner I am a Communist." Bridges the skeptical, conservative, comparatively wealthy aristocrat was so incensed he chose not to reply, and from August, 1871 to January, 1874—for close to two and a half years—no letters were exchanged. And even though in 1873 Hopkins was teaching rhetoric and poetry to scholastics in the Roehampton suburb of London, the friends did not meet.

So Hopkins was stunned when in January, 1874, he was reading an issue of the literary journal *The Academy* and found on page 53 a review of *Poems* by Robert Bridges, an author praised for "a fancy that can be strange when it chooses, and has always a power of delicate surprise, simplicity, courtliness, feeling, music of no vulgar order." The medical student had been so secretive about writing poetry that a hurt and somewhat humiliated Hopkins sent an affectionate letter wondering if this Robert Bridges was indeed his old friend. "Did I ever before see anything of yours?" Hopkins wrote. "I cannot remember."

Whether Bridges replied is uncertain. Ever concerned about his privacy, and possibly embarrassed by his snappish views, Bridges destroyed his side of the correspondence in his old age. But we can at least guess at Hopkins's chagrin over being kept in the dark about the poems, and the pang he must have felt at seeing his friend having accomplished what had long been for him not just a hobby but an aspiration.

The year before Hopkins was born, his father had published *The Philosopher's Stone and other poems*, and when Gerard was five his father and uncle collaborated on a book of poems entitled *Pietas Metrica*. At Highgate School, Gerard had won an exhibition scholarship to Oxford based on a prize poem entitled "The Escorial," on the martyrdom of Saint Lawrence, and describing in fifteen stanzas the conquest of a famous Spanish palace, monastery, and church. And at Oxford he'd written perhaps a hundred poems—including "Heaven-Haven," "Where art thou friend," and "The Habit of Perfection"—some of which he burned before joining the Society of Jesus, symbolically stating in that so-called "massacre of the innocents" that he'd given up one vocation for another. And yet he continually spoke about poetic form and diction when he and Bridges were together. Combined with his happiness over his friend's achievement there must have been a measure of envy and a worry that he had been superseded.

In December 1874, Bridges took his final written, oral, and clinical examinations in therapeutics, medicine, surgery, midwifery, forensic medicine, and hygiene, and the next month commenced work as house physician at Saint Bartholomew's Hospital in London with a salary of a paltry twenty-five pounds per annum, which would not have covered nine months' rent of a room at Oxford.

Hopkins was by then in northern Wales, at the theologate of Saint Beuno's, where his studies so preoccupied him that he recalled taking Aristotle's *Metaphysics* from the library shelf and promptly putting it back, recognizing there would be no free time in which to read it. And he still felt that poetry writing "would interfere with my state and vocation."

But then on December 7th, 1875, the *Deutschland*, a German emigrant ship steaming from Bremen to America, ran aground on a notoriously treacherous sandbank in the Thames Estuary, and fifty of the crew and passengers were drowned, including five Franciscan nuns who were exiled from their homeland by Bismarck's anti-Catholic laws.

The thirty-one-year old theology student later wrote that "I was affected by the account and, happening to say so to my rector, he said that he wished someone would write a poem on the subject. On this hint I set to work and, though my hand was out at first, produced one. I had long had haunting my ear the echo of a new rhythm which I now realized on paper."

In the thirty-five stanzas of "The Wreck of the Deutschland," Hopkins joined the heroic and allusive elements of the Greek choral ode with the then common genre of the sea-disaster poem that was popularized in 1839 by Henry Wadsworth Longfellow's "The Wreck of Hesperus." But its originality lay in the intricacies of its allegory and symbolism, the surprising vigor and invention of its vocabulary, and its haunting religious vision, in which Hopkins links himself, the five nuns, and Christ: each committed to serving others, and each accepting exile, desolation, and misery. Quite unlike Hopkins's lyric poems at Oxford, which seemed principally inspired by Keats, "The Wreck of the Deutschland" and the sonnets that were to follow it were experimental, passionate, non-imitative, and written in "sprung rhythm," a speech-based prosody which, as he wrote another poet, "consists in scanning by accents or stresses alone, without any account of the number of syllables."

Submitting the poem to the British Jesuit periodical *The Month*, Hopkins heard at first it was accepted for the July issue, but a subeditor was then asked to look at it, and he later recalled that "the only result was to give me a very bad headache, and to lead me to hand back the poem to Fr. Coleridge with the remark that it was indeed unreadable."

Stingingly rejected by his own community, Hopkins sought no other audience for "The Wreck of the Deutschland" until 1877 when Bridges sent him *Carmen Elegiacum*, a privately published Latin poem of farewell to a hospital mentor, along with a collection of twenty-four sonnets entitled *The Growth of Love*, about Doctor Bridges's wooing of a mystery woman who seems to have died unwon.

Weekly community encounters within the Society of Jesus, so-called "fraternal corrections," had instilled in Hopkins the invaluable gift of candor and he was frank in his criticisms, writing that parts of *Carmen Elegiacum* were "damned obscure" and that he looked upon its costly printing "as a waste of time and money." About *The Growth of Love* he was more encouraging. "In general I do not think that you have reached finality in point of execution, words might be chosen with more point and propriety, images might be more brilliant, etc." But he found a good deal of beauty in the book and generously praised Bridges for his "manly tenderness" and "flowing and never-failing music." As Jean-Georges Ritz points out, "it is remarkable to see how, from the very first letters in which Hopkins gives his opinion on Bridges's poems, he expresses himself with a masterly propriety. There is no conceit, no pride; the remarks are always to the point; but under the kindness or the abruptness lies the virile self-conviction of a teacher."

Included with his letter to Bridges was a handwritten copy of "The Wreck of the Deutschland," and Bridges bluntly responded to it with his own surly criticisms, finding fault with the poem's rhymes, the "presumptious jugglery" of its sprung rhythm—which he parodied—its oddity and obscurity, and the errors of taste in its metaphors. He added that no amount of money could persuade him to read the epic again.

The friendship might have been lastingly damaged by the critical exchange, but Hopkins replied to Bridges's letter with a tranquil mixture of wit, humility, and the sturdy confidence of genius, and when the Jesuit visited his family near London that summer, he and Bridges got together for a pleasant dinner, reminiscence, and serious conversations about poetry.

This was, after all, 1877, the *annus mirabilis* in Hopkins's life, the year not only of his September ordination to the priesthood, but of ten miraculous poems: "God's Grandeur," "The Starlight Night," "As kingfishers catch fire," "Spring," "The Sea and the Skylark," "In the Valley of the Elwy," "The Windhover," "Pied Beauty," "Hurrahing in Harvest," and "The Lantern out of Doors."

Robert Bridges's poetry starkly contrasted with those of his friend, both in his orthodox, archaic style, his metrical precision, and his skeptical, modernist themes. In *The Growth of Love*, for instance, Bridges confided his loss of faith in the sestet of "Sonnet 23," writing:

Dishearten'd pilgrims, I am one of you;

54

For, having worshipp'd many a barren face,
I scarce now greet the goal I journey'd to:
I stand a pagan in the holy place;
Beneath the lamp of truth I am found untrue,
  And question with the God that I embrace.

Even "Sonnet 69," so imitative of a contorted and antique prayer, is contaminated by dismay and despair:

Eternal Father, who didst all create,
In whom we live, and to whose bosom move,
To all men be Thy name known, which is Love,
Till its loud praises sound at heaven's high gate.
Perfect Thy kingdom in our passing state,
That here on earth Thou may'st as well approve
Our service, as Thou ownest theirs above,
Whose joy we echo and in pain await.

  Grant body and soul each day their daily bread:
And should in spite of grace fresh woe begin,
Even as our anger soon is past and dead
Be Thy remembrance mortal of our sin:
  By thee in paths of peace Thy sheep be led,
And in the vale of terror comforted.

Whereas Hopkins employed an unconventional vocabulary and metrical play to express, as in the sonnet "God's Grandeur," the electrical presence of the Holy Being immanent even in a denatured, industrial world, the consequence of sin and the means of atonement, the essential optimism of Christian faith, and the motherly love of God.

The world is charged with the grandeur of God.
It will flame out, like shining from shook foil;
It gathers to a greatness, like the ooze of oil
Crushed. Why do men then now not reck his rod?
Generations have trod, have trod, have trod;
And all is seared with trade; bleared, smeared with toil;
And wears man's smudge and shares man's smell: the soil
Is bare now, nor can foot feel, being shod.

And for all this, nature is never spent;
There lives the dearest freshness deep down things;
And though the last lights off the black West went
Oh, morning, at the brown brink eastward, springs—
Because the Holy Ghost over the bent

World broods with warm breast and with ah! bright wings.

English literature owes Robert Bridges a great debt for his responsible pasting of the handwritten poems into a blank book as he got them, for Hopkins himself was notoriously nonchalant about their preservation. But Bridges at first seemed to consider the poems the outlandish experiments of a crude amateur and was never wholly at ease with his friend's work. Sending the album of Hopkins's poetry to Coventry Patmore much later, Bridges inserted a note saying, "I have some misgivings lest I may have spoken too warmly of these poems, and prepared your mind for a disappointment . . . lest you should be ill-prepared for these poems I should tell you that Gerard Hopkins is affected in style. His affectation is somewhat natural to him, however, and subservient to general effect."

Writing of a selection in *The Poets and the Poetry of the Century* some years after Hopkins's death, Bridges again struggled to find anything good to say: "His early verse," he noted, "shows a mastery of Keatsian sweetness, but he soon developed a very different style of his own, so full of experiments in rhythm and diction that were his poems collected into one volume, they would appear as a unique effort in English literature. Most of his poems are religious, and marked with Catholic theology, and almost all are injured by a natural eccentricity, a love for subtlety and uncommonness, well denoted by the Greek term [extravagance, excess]. And this quality of mind hampered their author throughout life; for though to a fine intellect and varied accomplishments . . . he united humor, great personal charm, and the most attractive virtues of a tender and sympathetic nature—which won him love wherever he went and gave him zeal for his work—yet he was not considered publicly successful in his profession."

Even in his editorial notes in the collected *Poems* of 1918—which he titled identically to his own first book—Bridges could not forgive his friend's licenses. He wrote: "Apart from questions of taste—and if these poems were to be arraigned for errors of what may be called taste, they might be convicted of occasional affectation in metaphor . . . or of some perversion of human feeling . . . [T]hese and a few such examples are mostly efforts to force emotion into theological or sectarian channels . . . or, again, [there is] the exaggerated Marianism of some pieces, or the naked encounter of sensualism and asceticism." Bridges disliked "all the rude shocks of his purely artistic wantonness," "definite faults of style which a reader must have courage to face," and a disconcerting lack of "literary decorum."

Reading Bridges's notes on Hopkins's poems in 1920, a reviewer in *Poetry* exclaimed, "From our best friends, deliver us, O Lord!"

Because Bridges got rid of his half of the correspondence, we have only Hopkins's letters as a guide to their conversations on literature. We see in those letters that Hopkins could be just as merciless in his commentaries on Bridges's work, saying of Robert's play, *The Feast of Bacchus*, "The Menandrian period appears to me the dullest and narrowest world that one could choose to lay an action in, a jaded and faded civilization; moreover I have a craving for more brilliancy, more picturesque, more local colour: however you austerely set these things aside and I am to take the play for what it is. In its kind then, which has for me no attraction, and in its metre, which has to me no beauty, I think it a masterpiece."

More often we see the priest begging Bridges for heartening words: "I must absolutely have encouragement as much as crops rain." But he was quick to detect falseness or condescension: "It gave me of course great comfort to read your words of praise. But however, praise or blame, never mingle with your criticisms monstrous and indecent spiritual compliments." Quarreling with Bridges's finicky, old-fashioned qualms, Hopkins justified his poetry by stating with some prescience: "If the whole world agreed to condemn it or see nothing in it I should only tell them to take a generation and come to me again." And he reminded Bridges that he was the priest's sole audience: "You are my public and I hope to convert you."

"I hope to convert you" is, I think, a play on words: Hopkins implied he was trying to persuade Bridges of the beauty and propriety of his innovations, but crucially important to the Catholic priest was the state of Bridges's soul, for his Anglican faith was never orthodox and he seemed at times an atheist. And he was continually snide about Catholicism and the Jesuits, writing a friend about the posting of Hopkins to Oxford, "Whether he is actually sent to undermine the undergraduates steadily or not I cannot say."

While theirs seemed to be a denominational conflict between the Church of Rome and the Church of England, or between Catholicism and Protestantism, it was based in fact on the irreconcilable contrast between the Ignatian priest seeing God in all things and deeply concerned about our lives, and the Victorian scientist imagining the Holy Mystery at a great distance, coldly uninvolved, and either dead or dying. Hopkins, we shall see, sought to alter that view.

After his final year of theology and ordination in 1877, Hopkins held seven different jobs from London and Oxford to Liverpool and Glasgow, and then in 1881 was sent for tertianship—a sort of repetition of the Jesuit novice's first year—to Manresa House in Roehampton. There he and Doctor Bridges got together often in the gardens, but not without argument. In his long poem *The Testament of Beauty*, Bridges somewhat contemptuously recalled:

> ...And so,
> when the young poet my companion in study
> and friend of my heart refused a peach at my hands,
> he being then a housecarl in Loyola's menie,
> 'twas that he fear'd the savor of it, and when he waived
> his scruple to my banter, 'twas to avoid offence.

"Housecarl" is Middle English for a household soldier or bodyguard. "Menie" derives from the Middle English for underling or lackey. In other words, Bridges stole a peach from the garden at Manresa House, and when Hopkins, an Ignatian stooge, huffily refused it, Bridges understood it as a stickler's suppression of normal sensual pleasure.

One week later, Bridges attended a Corpus Christi procession in which Father Hopkins was a celebrant and seems to have spoken disdainfully of it, for Hopkins rejoined,

> ...it is long since such things had any significance for you. But what is strange and unpleasant is that you sometimes speak as if they had in reality none for me and you were only waiting with a certain disgust till I too should be disgusted with myself enough to throw off the mask. You said something of the sort walking on the Cowley Road when we were last at Oxford together—in '79 it must have been. Yet I can hardly think you do not think I am in earnest. And let me say, to take no higher ground, that without earnestness there is nothing sound or beautiful in character and that a cynical vein much indulged coarsens everything in us. Not that you do overindulge this vein in other matters: why then does it bulk out in that diseased and varicose way in this?

When a mutual friend at Oxford left the Catholic Church in 1888, having converted the year before Hopkins did, Bridges told the priest he was glad. To which Hopkins replied, "But why should you be glad? Why at any rate should you burst upon me that you are glad, when you know that I cannot be glad?" Even after Hopkins's death, Bridges was crass enough to write Hopkins's sister and say of his friend's melancholy and his Roman Catholic faith that "medievalizing does not always produce complete ease of mind."

Constrained and silenced on matters of religious faith that were so significant to himself, it may be that Hopkins sought to evangelize Bridges through his poetry, which joined missiology, the Christian vocation to be witnesses to Christ to all the ends of the earth, with mystagogy, instruction about the religious mysteries. "God's Grandeur," "The Windhover," and "Pied Beauty" are all examples of the analogical imagination that finds divinity expressing itself in "the dearest freshness," in "the mastery" of a falcon's flight, in "all things counter, original, spare, strange."

Look, too, at "Felix Randal" in which the priest wrote of a "hardy-handsome" farrier who was felled by four health disorders. Doctor Bridges, who was then working on the Saint Bartholomew's Hospital Casualty Ward, could not help but identify with the line, "This seeing the sick endears them to us, us too it endears." Of the blacksmith, Hopkins writes:

> Sickness broke him. Impatient, he cursed at first, but mended
> being anointed and all; though a heavenlier heart began some
> Months earlier, since I had our sweet reprieve and ransom
> Tendered to him.

Imitating Christ who, in the Gospel of Mark, sought first to forgive the sins of a paralyzed man in Capernaum before curing him of his infirmity, Father Hopkins healed the ailing soul of Felix Randal with the anointing of the sick and the sacrament of the Eucharist, "our sweet reprieve and ransom," rather than healing the body with diagnosis and medicine, as physicians do.

The instruction of the poem could not have been lost on Doctor Bridges. Indeed, "The Lantern out of Doors," "The Loss of the Eurydice," "The May Magnificat," "The Bugler's First Communion," "The Blessed Virgin Compared to the Air We Breathe," "That Nature is a Heraclitean Fire and of the Comfort of the Resurrection," and "In Honour of St.

Alphonsus Rodriguez," were like a patient and uninterrupted catechism, may have even seemed to Bridges an irritating, schoolmasterish assault, as they reminded the physician of a Trinity, a heaven, and a way of living that he no longer believed in.

Chiding him in a letter, Hopkins noted, "As I am criticizing you, so does Christ, only more correctly and more affectionately, both as a poet and as a man."

The twentieth-century American poet Wallace Stevens thought that "In an age of disbelief, or, what is the same thing, in a time that is largely humanistic, in one sense or another, it is for the poet to supply the satis-factions of belief, in his measure and in his style." Bridges strove to carry that out, but Hopkins would have scoffed at such a feeble and insufficient pursuit, for he knew that even the grandest poetry was a pale, scrappy, ephemeral description, a mere glimmer, of an immensely grander real-ity. Art and religion were for him conjoined in their efforts to give praise and glory to God, and Hopkins's poems are vital for us now in ways that his friend's are not because of the Spirit-fired certitude with which he ex-pressed what he had learned of the Great Mystery, sensually and in prayer.

In 1884, at the age of forty, Robert Bridges retired from medicine, married a Quaker, and retreated to a manor at Yattendon, near Oxford, where he lived calmly but industriously with his contentments of litera-ture and music. Within a few years he would be nominated for the Chair of Poetry at Oxford—which he declined—and in 1912 he, with Henry James, was awarded an Honorary Doctor of Literature there. By then reviewers were so extolling him as the greatest living master of English verse, that it was no surprise when Prime Minister Asquith passed over Rudyard Kipling to name Robert Bridges Poet Laureate of Great Britain in 1913.

Whereas in 1884, the still unpublished Father Hopkins was sent to Dublin, Ireland, where he would spend the final five exhausting years of his life as an examiner in the classics in the newly formed Catholic Uni-versity College. The rift between him and Bridges widened and his last melancholy poems, "Justus quidem tu es, Domine" and "To R.B.," seem to try to explain himself, his needs, and his hopes for their friendship. But in May, 1889, Bridges heard the priest was ill with fever and wrote a solicitous letter to "Dearest Gerard," praying he recover quickly. On June

8th Gerard Hopkins died. The cause has long been said to be typhoid, but that may have been a misdiagnosis, for the symptoms also resemble those of Crohn's disease or some other intestinal illness.

Writing of his death to a mutual friend, Bridges stated in a footnote, "that dear Gerard was overworked, unhappy & would never have done anything great seems to give no solace. But how much worse it wd have been had his promise or performance been more splendid. He seems to have been entirely lost & destroyed by those Jesuits."

Bridges's mother was gentler, writing to Mrs. Hopkins, "I looked upon him always as a Holy spiritual, more than an Earthly being, and I loved to know and feel he was Robert's real friend."

But when, in 1909, *Catholic World* published Katherine Brégy's "Gerard Hopkins: An Epitaph and Appreciation," Bridges sent the essay to Mrs. Hopkins with the resistant, dismissive, envious note that "The Catholics are very hard up for any literary interests, and are glad enough to make something of Gerard's work." And when, four months later, the English Jesuit Joseph Keating sought to use Hopkins's poems in a series of articles, Bridges was again obstructive, writing to Mrs. Hopkins, "I do not think Gerard wd have wished his poems to be edited by a committee of those fellows," and "I am sure they wd make a dreadful mess of the whole thing." Even when *Poems* by Gerard Manley Hopkins was finally issued, and in its second year of publication sold a third more copies than in its first, Bridges scoffed, "Truly the world is upside down—and its rump is not altogether beautiful."

I have a hard time not being hard on Doctor Bridges, but the fact is he was Hopkins's closest friend, his confidante, his "Dearest Bridges," and in spite of his meanness, prejudices, and haughtiness toward Hopkins, he did indeed have deep affection for his friend. In spite of their religious differences, it may have been the peculiar chemistry of their literary companionship that inspired some of the greatest religious poetry since George Herbert and John Donne. And we have Robert Bridges to thank for finally having the *Poems* published nearly thirty years after his friend died.

Bridges was the grand man of English letters then and could not have foreseen how interest in his own poetry would languish just as interest in that of Gerard Manley Hopkins would grow. But he was touched and perhaps graced with misgivings when he was mistakenly sent Hopkins's spiritual journal from his final retreat and read his dearest Gerard's private note that, "Also in some med[itation]s today I earnestly asked our Lord to watch over my compositions . . . [that] they might do me no harm through the enmity or imprudence of any man or my own; that he would have them as his own and employ or not employ them as he should see fit. And this I believe is heard."

# A COLLISION OF SYSTEMS AND TENDENCIES

## George Tyrrell

HE WAS BORN IN DUBLIN IN 1861, THE FOURTH CHILD OF ENGLISH parents Mary Chamney and William Henry Tyrrell, a journalist with the *Evening Mail,* the foremost Protestant-Tory newspaper in Ireland. William was talented but ill-tempered and domineering, and he left his family penniless when he died two months before George's birth. Thence forward Mary and the four children were vagabonds, shifting homes and schools sometimes two or three times in a single year. Witty, friendly, if often aloof, George found friends at school but thought their games, so governed by rules, a form of humbuggery and sought instead the wilder excitements of, as he put it, "gymnastics and fighting and tearing about, and climbing and courting danger."

At the age of eight, he enrolled in Rathmines School and found such ease and success in his classes that he succumbed to what he later recognized as flaws of character: "first, a confirmed habit of idleness; secondly, an overweening conceit of my own powers." But it was there that his headmaster acquainted him with an Evangelical, High Church Anglicanism that fascinated him but left him skeptical and basically godless until he met Anne Kelly, a Roman Catholic and the Tyrrell's maid-of-all-work whose kitchen became his after-school haunt. Lovesickness caused him to defend her against the fervent Protestant accusations of his mother and he felt an "anxiety to say something in favour of so preposterous a religion as Popery; while my secret unbelief made me find little objection to the gnats of Romanism after the camels of Christianity."

Ever more entranced by a Catholicism that he found "dangerous, wicked and forbidden," George first tried a religious half-measure of secretly attending a Church of Ireland where the ministers wore birettas and cassocks and instead of a communion table there was an altar of sacrifice. With feelings of sinful mischief, George hid crucifixes and images of saints in his room, slept on a board, and flagellated himself with a handmade discipline in a fantastic impersonation of faith that fixed on extremes of piety but had nothing to do with the spirit.

Uprooted again, the family rented a furnished apartment from a Miss Lynch, a Roman Catholic landlady whom George adored, and, as he confessed in his autobiography, "This quiet, holy, unselfish little woman had more to do with my destiny than any other" force.

Within a half-year, George's agnostic brother Willie, who was not yet twenty-five, died following a sudden, desperate illness. Rocked by the tragedy, his fifteen-year-old brother flung himself into hagiographies and histories, including Charles Montalembert's six-volume *Monks of the West*. Reading Compline in Latin one night, he found himself praying to Saint Benedict "straight in the teeth of my Protestant conscience, " and when his eyes fell back on the page of his Latin breviary, he read the concluding verses of Psalm 91: "Because he hoped in me, I will deliver him; I will protect him, because he hath known my name; he shall cry out to me, and I will hear him; I am with him in tribulation, I will deliver him, and I will glorify him."

Having failed a sizarship examination that would have granted him free tuition to Trinity College in Dublin, George felt excused to sail to England to help the poor of the city slums, but with an ulterior notion of religious conversion and even, perhaps, ordination to the priesthood. And fortuitously, in a London bookshop, he happened upon Paul Feval's *Jesuits* and recalled how Miss Lynch once counseled him to join the Society of Jesus, for "they are very learned and very holy men." With that in mind, he took catechetical instruction from a Jesuit in the Farm Street residence in Mayfair, and on Sunday, May 18th, 1879, George Tyrrell was received into the Roman Catholic Church.

He was eighteen then, blond, frail, and homely, with a face like a caricature, but with a winsome goodness, intellect, and sincerity that earned him the sympathy and affection of others. Jesuits at Farm Street urged him at once to join their Order, but canon law forbad a convert from entering religious life for at least a year. The English province superior therefore sent Tyrrell to work on a Jesuit mission in Cyprus as a lay volunteer, and then to the English College in Malta where some Jesuits treated the convert "not as one who had courageously embraced a more difficult and somewhat paradoxical position, in lieu of an easier and more obvious one; but rather as a drunkard who had come to his senses—a repentant fool, if not a repentant rake."

Yet, with some misgivings, in September 1880 Tyrrell entered the Jesuit novitiate in the pastoral southwest London suburb of Roehampton, and there he was forever changed by the *Spiritual Exercises* of Saint Ignatius Loyola, the founder of the Society of Jesus. The purpose of those four weeks of silence and contemplation on the mysteries of the Trinity, humanity's sin, and the life, death, and resurrection of Christ was to free the new Jesuit from addictions and worldly attachments, to help him develop an intimate friendship with Jesus, to avail himself of deeply personal mystical graces, and to choose rightly, based on Ignatius's rules for discernment of the spirits of good and evil. Those and other retreat experiences would be found imprinted on each page of Tyrrell's future writing. But also incipient then were his dissatisfaction with a hollow, mechanistic asceticism and an inflexible, irrational orthodoxy. Each would prove to be his undoing some years hence.

Still, in 1882 he professed his first vows of poverty, chastity, and obedience as a Jesuit, and he was sent up to Stonyhurst College in Lancashire ahead of his class for philosophical studies that his superiors hoped would focus his restless mind. But instead of the favored neo-scholastic *interpretation* of Thomas Aquinas by the 16th-century Spanish Jesuit Francisco Suárez, happenstance permitted Tyrrell to concentrate enthusiastically on the Thomistic sources themselves. And the lazy, often indifferent scholar fell in love with learning while earning the confidence and praise of Jesuit professors who hailed him as the finest mind in his class.

His philosophate was completed in 1885, and for his regency he requested a return to the English College in Malta where he taught elementary schoolboys for a fulfilling three years. His final education as a seminarian was at the Jesuit theologate of St. Beuno's in North Wales—where Gerard Manley Hopkins had matriculated fourteen years earlier—and at last, at age thirty, George Tyrrell, SJ, was ordained a priest of Christ by the Bishop of Shrewsbury.

His first apostolate was at Saint Aloysius parish in Oxford, followed by a quick reassignment to an intellectually backward and financially strapped congregation in Lancashire's coal country that would surprisingly offer him the happiest year of his life. In those hectic days of the ever-growing English Province, few Jesuits stayed on a job long—Hopkins shifted houses so frequently that he called himself "fortune's football"—so, too soon and against his wishes, Tyrrell was given a chair in philosophy at Stonyhurst College, where he'd been judged a rising star nine years earlier. He was thirty-three.

Eloquent, incisive, challenging, and clever, he was a natural as a teacher, exciting in his thought, accessible and pastoral with his students, ever self-effacing, but also humorously sardonic about his far less popular fellow professors and their stiff fidelity to Suárez rather than the originator of his teaching, Thomas Aquinas. Within just two years Tyrrell had won the love and loyalty of the seminarians but the envy and enmity of faculty who feared, he told a relative, that, "I was turning the young men into Dominicans."

It was determined he could not stay.

Looking for a happier spot for him, his Jesuit superiors decided to fit him into the staff of editors on the Jesuit journal *The Month*, headquartered at Farm Street, so he could occupy himself full-time with writing. Even in the theologate of Saint Beuno's he'd been fluent and tireless with his pen, often filling whole holidays with trenchant papers—three articles ran in *The Month* but some others were jests and opinions meant only for his classmates—on a stunningly wide array of topics, from biblical criticism to socialism to the harm in cramming for exams. And now he was given free license to publish and a friendly, if vigilant, journal for his many lucubrations.

At first there were cogent, often generous, but increasingly acidic reviews of theological and philosophical texts, then a series of rather quarrelsome articles on Anglicanism that some Roman ecclesiastics possibly smiled on, and he even shuffled up two collections of intellectual catechesis and piety—*Nova et Vera* and *Hard Sayings: A Selection of Meditations and Studies*—intended for the enrichment of highly educated Catholics.

Still smarting over his ejection from Stonyhurst, he was cautious about rousting his censors.

Then in 1899 he delivered a series of eight Lenten lectures to the Roman Catholic undergraduates at Oxford University, which he published in book form as *External Religion: Its Use and Abuse*. His Jesuit superiors found no reason to censure the book but it would arouse the vigilance of the Holy See because he spoke of the Church not as a fine philosophical construct nor a majestic political force, but as a *sacrament* intended by Christ to help and grace human beings.

Maude Petre, Tyrrell's good friend and first biographer, wrote: "The Church for him was a lowlier, and yet, in the best sense, holier creation, standing on the ground, at the level of the weakest, its doors wide open, its pavement soiled by the feet of the poor and miserable; ready to learn, even while she taught, to serve while she commanded." She had long been an *Ecclesia docens*, a Church teaching, but she needed also to be an *Ecclesia discens*, a Church learning.

Tyrrell continued to publish widely, often at the rate of two books per year. *The Faith of Millions* was a collection of meditations inspired by his prayer with the *Spiritual Exercises* and the book called for, in part, a greater appreciation of the vital and telling religious experiences of ordinary Christians.

Writing to a friend about his work on *The Church of the Future*, Tyrrell noted that, "I make the saints and not the theologians the teachers of Christianity. The Spirit of Christ rather than Christ Himself is the creator of the Church."

Tyrrell considered *Lex Orandi, or Prayer and Creed*, a book of pastoral theology on our human longing for a transcendent God. Tyrrell noted in his preface, "That we are dissatisfied, not only with what the ideal gives us, but, by anticipation, with all it could ever possibly give us, is proof that there is a higher love-power within us which must seek its object elsewhere."

The title came from the Latin saying, "Lex orandi, lex credendi," which can be translated: "As the Church prays, so she believes."

And so he next wrote the sequel, *Lex Credendi*, in which he argued that the Spirit of Christ depicted in the Gospels was also revealed in the lives of the saints, all adapting the Spirit to their own time and place and providing a guide for the Church's "really fruitful and lasting decisions. . . . The Pope is in theory no irresponsible absolutist who can define what he likes, who can make truth and unmake it. He is but the interpreter of a law written by the Holy Ghost in the hearts of the saints. He is bound by this living book."

Even the section titles of Tyrrell's *The Church of the Future* hints at disputations that the Holy See could not overlook: "Catholicism as Officially Stated; or, the Theory of Ecclesiastical Inerrancy"; "A Liberal Restatement of Catholicism"; and "The Ethics of Conformity." What Tyrrell was arguing throughout was that the deposit of faith was a Spirit, an Idea, that grew organically and changed over time, and only holiness was proof for deciding whether conscience and religious experience truly conformed to the Spirit of Christ.

All his ideas were incendiary to ecclesiastics only a century removed from the slaughter of clergy and religious during the French Revolution. They saw Marxism on the rise across the Continent; priests and seminarians executed or expelled from Spain during the *"gloriosa revolución"* of 1868; anti-clericalism becoming public policy in Otto von Bismarck's Reich; there was, as the Holy See called it, "a ferocious war against the Church" in South America; and enflaming the memories of those in the Roman hierarchy was the recent seizure of the wealthy Papal States by the Italian Army, with the result that the only sovereign entity of the papacy became the Apostolic Palace and the loop of fortifications on Vatican Hill.

The *ecclesia docens* felt under siege.

An initial response was the *Syllabus of Errors* issued by Pope Pius IX. ("The ninth" in Italian is *"nono,"* so wags were soon calling him "Papa Nono.") The Syllabus was subdivided into ten sections in which a host of false statements were made and then condemned by citing earlier papal documents that had considered that error. So, for example, "All truths of religion proceed from the innate strength of human reason," or "Protestantism is nothing more than another form of the same true Christian religion," or "The Roman Pontiff can, and ought to, reconcile himself, and come to terms with, progress, liberalism, and modern civilization."

In the squint of ecclesiastical prejudice and suspicion, Tyrrell's intricate philosophy of religion would be corrupted and misconstrued until it seemed in itself a syllabus of such errors. But accusations became more telling with Pius X's 1907 decree *Lamentabili sane exitu* ("With Truly Deplorable Results") by which the Holy Office condemned and proscribed sixty-five errors of Modernists in biblical exegesis and the interpretation of the mysteries of the faith.

Without naming the offenders, the Holy Office left little doubt that it was condemning and consigning to the Index of Forbidden Books the biblical criticism of Alfred Loisy, a French Catholic priest and professor of Hebrew who maintained, for instance, that the first five chapters of Genesis are only figurative history, that Moses was not the author of the Pentateuch, that scripture shares the problems and limitations of all other ancient texts, and that Jesus did not intend an organized Church.

And of course *Lamentabili* was also meant to anathematize the writing of George Tyrrell. Soon after reading it, he sent a confidential letter to his superior general in Rome, the Spanish Jesuit Luis Martín, offering to formally request release from the Society of Jesus, which he felt was "leagued with those who are doing everything to make faith impossible."

Already he'd left Farm Street and his work on *The Month* for the rustic tranquility of a small Jesuit parish in Yorkshire's Richmond-in-Swaledale where his job was to simply be a good priest, and it would consume a full two years of worrying over his Jesuit status before he finally received his dismissal from the Order, with the conditions that he could receive communion but not celebrate Mass, and that he could be reinstated to priestly ministry and the Society of Jesus only through formal applications.

Tyrrell wrote Luis Martín that, "I shd. like to assure you, now that I stand outside the Society, how completely I realize that we have both of us been driven to this unpleasant issue by the necessities of our several minds & consciences; & Y[our] P[aternity] still more by the exigencies of a most difficult position. . . . Nothing cd. be further from my sentiments than any sort of personal rancour or resentment. I feel that it is a collision of systems & tendencies rather than of persons; & that many such collisions must occur before the truth of both sides meets some higher truth."

Even as he was seeking a way to reestablish himself as a priest by consenting to censorship of his writing, Pope Pius X issued his September 1907 encyclical *Pascendi Dominici Gregis* ("Feeding the Lord's Flock"), which focused even more militantly on those deemed Modernists, condemning their teaching as the "compendium of all heresies," calling them "enemies of the Church," and viciously describing these still unnamed theologians in terms generally applied to Satan.

Tyrrell felt the need to comment and did so in an extensive letter to the London *Times* that was printed in two installments. Writing of the encyclical, he claimed, "As an argument it falls dead for every one who regards its science theory as obsolete; for all who believe that truth has not been stagnating for centuries in theological seminaries, but has been steadily streaming on, with ever increasing force and volume, in the channels which liberty has opened to its progress." Noting that it was not a statement *ex cathedra*—that is, infallible—he called it "a disciplinary measure preceded by a catena of the personal opinions of Pius X and his immediate *entourage*." Any "modernist," he wrote, could now expect censure, suspension, and excommunication. "They were the portion of his spiritual ancestors, who in past ages so often saved the Church, sick unto death with the pedantries of scholastic rationalism and the *rabies theologorum*" [madness of theologians]. And just when the people were hoping that the Church "might have bread for the starving millions, for those who are troubled by that vague hunger for God on which the Encyclical pours such scorn . . . Pius X comes forth with a stone in one hand and a scorpion in the other."

Recognizing that there would be dire consequences for an ordained priest who publicly rebuked the Holy Father, Tyrrell was not surprised to hear in October 1907 that he'd been given a "minor" excommunication. Afterward he was frequently urged to rejoin the Anglicans, but Tyrrell would not, for, "I feel my work is to hammer away at the great unwieldy carcass of the Roman Communion and wake it up from its medieval dreams."

He was a houseguest of friends in Clapham when, in 1909, he fell seriously ill with a kidney malady that was later correctly diagnosed as the final stages of Bright's disease. Even from his sickbed he produced *Christianity at the Cross-Roads*, a book that avoided criticism of Roman Catholicism to instead examine its riches and use it as a comparative measure of other religious expressions. In it he wrote, "It is impossible to deny that the revelation of the Catholic religion and that of Jesus are the same. . . . It was in the form of such a tradition that He necessarily embodied His

Gospel, and the Catholic Church has preserved the earthen vessel with its heavenly treasure."

After signing the preface to the book in June, he went to Maude Petre's home in Storrington and fell critically ill with a stroke that paralyzed his left side and garbled his speech. A friendly priest was called in and heard Tyrrell's confession, and just before headaches, nausea, and internal bleeding finally rendered Tyrrell comatose, another priest, who'd been hostile toward him from the pulpit, found the pastoral grace to administer the sacrament of Extreme Unction.

On July 15th, 1909, George Tyrrell died at age forty-eight.

Rome issued instructions that he should be denied the Catholic funeral rites, so after fruitless appeals to the bishops of Southwark and Westminster, his friends Maude Petre and Baron Friedrich von Hügel arranged for a burial in Storrington in the Anglican churchyard. Henri Bremond, a French former Jesuit and modernist, but still a priest with full faculties, recited the familiar prayers over Tyrrell's coffin and gave a eulogy that ended: "To realise that we shall never hear him again on earth would entirely darken our lives, if he had not taught us his own bitter, but triumphant, optimism and the present duty of hoping against hope. Hope! This must be our parting word and feelings."

In 1910, Pius X signed a *motu proprio* insisting that all clerics in major orders and professors on Catholic faculties of philosophy and theology swear an oath against modernism. In 1912 Maude Petre published *The Autobiography and Life of George Tyrrell* and soon saw the two volumes placed on the Index of Forbidden Books.

High ecclesiastical authorities may have gloated that they'd annihilated the life and writings of George Tyrrell, but as David G. Schultenover, SJ points out in *George Tyrrell: In Search of Catholicism*, "Anyone who has studied both him and the documents of Vatican II will recognize his principles reborn on nearly every page. Thus was fulfilled the prophecy that Tyrrell applied to himself and inscribed in his breviary" when he left the philosophate at Stonyhurst. It was a lesson first given to Moses: "Thou shalt see from afar the land which the Lord God will give to the children of Israel, but thou shalt not enter therein."

II

# FICTION AS ENCOUNTER
## An Interview with Brennan O'Donnell

**Brennan O'Donnell**: Your new novel, *Exiles,* explores the shipwreck that inspired Gerard Manley Hopkins's long poem *The Wreck of the Deutschland,* as well as Hopkins's writing of that poem. How did you come to write a novel about an English Jesuit's poem about a German shipwreck?

**Ron Hansen**: Like a lot of people, I happened onto Hopkins. I found out that Dylan Thomas, whom I admired, was a fan of Hopkins and had learned a lot from him. The more you dig into Hopkins, the more fascinating he becomes. You can go back to the poems again and again and see new things, which is a mark of his genius.

I'd always had difficulty with *The Wreck of the Deutschland,* just at the level of figuring out what's going on, so I started researching. When I discovered the story of the real shipwreck, I thought it would be a great idea for a story. I happened to mention it to Joe Feeney, who runs the *Hopkins Quarterly,* and he told me about a new book that assembled a lot of the newspaper accounts of the incident. That book really stimulated my thinking. Then I found out about the Wheaton Franciscans, who are the vestiges of the group of nuns on board. I contacted a sister there who had translated a book from the German about the shipwreck called *The Floundering Rescue.* I started assembling information about the events, how the ship was built, everything I could find out about shipwrecks on the east coast of England. Then I started imagining the lives of these five Franciscan nuns. There's not much known about them. I thought at first I was just writing a story about the shipwreck, but as I looked at the poem again and again, I realized that the shipwreck itself, and the sense of exile that the young nuns felt, were really metaphors for Hopkins's own life. He felt cut off not only from Oxford and from his parents, but from England itself, especially when he went to Ireland just before he died.

I wanted to deal with the question of how people encounter death, their various attitudes toward it and toward God's way of dealing with people. Why is it that some people lead wonderful lives and have terrible deaths? Why, as the psalmist asks, do the evil prosper and the innocent suffer? All of that is wound up in the novel.

**BO**: Were you particularly fascinated with Hopkins responding to these events as a writer?

**RH**: I was interested in this idea of reputation: Hopkins was an unknown poet during his lifetime. People thought he was an eccentric nut, but thirty years later his book got published and he became famous, a bestseller. What does that say about our sense of trust in God? What does that say to you, in this day, as a writer, about your sense of reputation and of doing God's will? Hopkins once wrote to a canon who was also a poet, "Christ is the only literary critic." What does he mean by that? That's the thing I was trying to explore in the novel.

**BO**: What most surprised you as you got deeper and deeper into the research, both about Hopkins and about the German nuns?

**RH**: I found that Hopkins's famous poems of desolation really came from a discrete period in his life, a period he showed every evidence of coming out of. There's strong evidence that he was a manic depressive, at least at some point in his life. In his letters from Ireland you see shifts between frenetic activity and incredible desolation. But in the very last poems you don't see the desolation you see in his earlier work. This makes me wonder, what would have happened if he'd gone on, if he hadn't fallen ill in Dublin? What kinds of poems would have come, what kind of essays? He had all kinds of projects that never came to fruition. We only have this one collection of poems, and even that was really shaped by Robert Bridges.

**BO**: What most surprised you about the shape the novel took as it progressed? When you were first writing it, you described it as being based on a fascination you had with the correspondence of Hopkins and Robert

Bridges, but that changed over time. How did that affect the structure of the book?

**RH**: I did think at one point of doing a whole life of Hopkins, starting from the time he enters Oxford. Bridges would have been a crucial character. But I got seventeen pages in and hadn't even started his first day of classes. I had no way of focusing. I needed some kind of device to limit what I was going to say. Otherwise it was too comprehensive a novel. Everything I have to say about Hopkins in *Exiles* in some way touches on *The Wreck of the Deutschland*. Either he's talking to somebody about the poem, or he's getting counsel from Bridges, or he's being exiled in some way. That became my way of selection.

Also, I wrote an essay about Hopkins and Bridges, and that remedied some of my yearnings. I use some of that essay in the book. I'm not a big fan of Bridges. I think he was one of those friends who in some subtle way undermine you. Nobody reads Bridges anymore, but at that time he was famous enough to become poet laureate of England, which tells you something about that culture. And Hopkins couldn't get published anywhere at that time, which tells you something else about that culture. The fact that Hopkins finally wins out fills me with glee.

**BO**: While you were writing *Exiles,* your good friend Paul Mariani was hard at work on his biography of Hopkins. How did your friendship begin? Did you two compare notes as you wrote your books?

**RH**: Paul and I first met in 1980 at Breadloaf in the faculty lounge. He sidled over to me and said, "I heard somebody say that you're a Catholic," and I said, "Yes, I am." He said, "Tomorrow is the Feast of the Assumption. Do you want to go to mass with me?" and I said yes. So we were secret Catholics together.

Paul and I did a retreat together at Saint Beuno's in Wales, where Hopkins studied theology. Paul was working on the biography and I was working on the novel, and we wanted to see what life was like there, so we did a six-day retreat.

We corresponded while I was working on the novel. Whenever I was stumped I would write him, and he would have an answer for me in a couple of hours. When I started the book, he sent me files of all of Hopkins's correspondence and journal entries, along with his own parenthetical notes about who everybody was. I couldn't have found that stuff myself, so I'm deeply grateful.

**BO**: In 1996, you accepted the Gerard Manley Hopkins chair at Santa Clara University. How did that come about?

**RH**: I did some of my first writing about Hopkins while I was getting my MA in spirituality from Santa Clara. I started taking classes there while I was a professor at the University of California at Santa Cruz, from 1989 to 1995. During that time I got to know Father Paul Locatelli, the president of Santa Clara. A couple had recently endowed a new chair but didn't want it named after themselves. Father Locatelli offered me the job, but I wasn't sure whether to take it. I decided to pray to Gerard Manley Hopkins about the decision, since I thought he knew my life. A little later Father Locatelli called me up and asked if I'd decided, and I said no. He said, "I'm going to name it the Gerard Manley Hopkins Chair. Does that mean anything to you?" It was like Saint Paul being knocked off the horse.

**BO**: Could you talk about the connection between the Spiritual Exercises of Saint Ignatius and your imaginative life?

**RH**: The Spiritual Exercises are based on Ignatian contemplation, where you read a passage of scripture and then open it up by drawing out the events in your imagination, either starting earlier or going later than the passage does. You develop a more sensual experience of the event. Ignatius will often ask you to take the point of view of different people. You might be the person who was born blind. You might be a person looking on. You might be Jesus himself. As you expand the story, often it goes to something particular about your own life. After you've been healed, you might ask Jesus, "You've healed my eyesight, now what about this other issue?" It becomes a way of personal communication.

And that, I think, is what literature does. Writers try to make things as sensual as possible so that readers really enter into the scene and then learn something. You learn people's theology or philosophy in how they encounter other people, how they face crises. Writing and Ignatian contemplation use the same skill.

**BO**: You've described yourself as a "sifter through old, dusty tomes." What attracts you about writing about the past? Is there a connection between Ignatian contemplation and writing historical fiction?

**RH**: There's a lot of remembering in historical fiction. For example, you have to remember that there are no lights after six o'clock at night unless you have a candle or a kerosene lamp. Or that the kitchens aren't attached to the house. When Hopkins wakes up in the morning, he uses a chamber pot. You're constantly backing up and saying, "Oh, wait a second, they would have been barefoot, wouldn't they?" Those little things are important, and Ignatian contemplation makes you aware of that.

Part of the reason I write historical fiction is that I think people are impoverished in their historical imagination, and I want to bring out what these earlier lives were like. Also, a writer can own the past in a way that you can't own the present. If I write about contemporary circumstances, everybody thinks they know all about them already. Whereas there is a sort of suspension of disbelief that comes when you accept that I know more than you do about how trains ran in the 1870s.

**BO**: You've said that historical fiction is always as much about the time in which it is written as about the time in which it was set. What is it about 2008 that informs the world of *Exiles*?

**RH**: I have a sense that members of religious orders are still ostracized. A lot of people would prefer the orders leave the United States, and the same was true then in Germany. I think persecution is going to increase over the years.

It's not easy for writers of faith today. People do question whether you should write about such things. When I was first writing *Mariette in Ecstasy*, I asked one of my editors what he would think of a novel about a nun, and he just turned his thumbs down. I told him that was what I was working on, and he said, "Oh, well, you. That's different." Robert Bridges, in his introduction to Hopkins's collection, writes that a lot of the poems offend him because they deal with "cultish" things like Mary and so on. The questions Hopkins was facing in his day were the same ones a writer faces now. The fact that there was a panel at the Associated Writing Programs conference on the problems of poets dealing with faith seems kind of anomalous when you consider that all poetry and fiction came out of religious tradition. It used to be that all you would write about was God and man. Some think that if you do that now you're either breaching good taste or you've lost your mind.

**BO**: You've written that the phenomenon of the stigmata seems "grossly old fashioned" to modern sensibilities. Why center a novel on something grossly old fashioned?

**RH**: It's the nature of novels to deal with problems. And the problems have to be made tangible in some way. Mariette having a crisis of faith is not very interesting, but if the crisis has a physical manifestation that brings in the quarrels between science and religion, the book has more possibilities. The stigmata awaken either revulsion or awe in other nuns in her coterie. This is a sign that cannot be manufactured, or shouldn't be, and it raises questions: Why is she privileged and I'm not, when I'm as holy as she is? All kinds of rivalries arise, and then there's the problem of hysteria. This is the meat of novels.

**BO**: Among other things, the novel demonstrates the challenge of the stigmata to a sensibility that is inclined to be open to the miraculous. What is it about miracles that we find so troubling, even we people of faith?

**RH**: We expect miracles of Jesus, but we don't expect them in contemporary life. It feels almost like a reproach to the Gospels that miracles should happen now, and people will bend over backwards to try to find a practical or materialistic explanation, even people who are very devout, very spiritually aware.

In researching *Mariette*, I read everything I could about the stigmata. It was especially popular as a subject in the nineteenth century. In virtually every case, it was divisive. Each time, there was a block of people who thought it was phony, and another block who thought it was real. Sometimes the people who got the stigmata weren't religious at all and were embarrassed by it. Some were ignorant of it, and were told by doctors, "If I didn't know better I'd say this was the stigmata."

For the novel, I made up my own religious order so I could get away with things, so I didn't have to follow the exact rule of the Dominicans or the Benedictines, but the story does follow closely what happened to several of the nuns I read about, chiefly Gemma Galgani.

The stigmata awaken a lot of questions. Why does this happen to some people and not to others? It appears in Francis of Assisi and the famous Franciscan Padre Pio. What is it about Franciscan spirituality that causes it? And why is it that the most contemplative orders have the fewest stigmatics?

**BO**: At the center of *Mariette in Ecstasy* is a powerful blending of religious fervor and eroticism. Can you talk a bit about what you think the novel may contribute to our understanding of that volatile combination?

**RH**: In a spirituality class at Santa Clara, I heard a woman say that a problem she had was that her love for Jesus got mixed up with romantic love. My wife once said that on a retreat, whenever she started thinking about Jesus, he became Jeremy Irons, and they would start dancing together. Another woman once told me that the problem is that the body's vocabulary is very limited, and feelings of deep love become sensual very quickly.

In the novel, I wanted to show how these things are connected. I think it's no accident that priests and ministers so often get into trouble because of romantic involvement. It's not that religion and sex are opposed to one another; it's that they're inextricably linked. That's one of the secrets that I wanted to have out.

Sometimes *Mariette in Ecstasy* does end up in the erotic section of bookstores, which is amusing to me. An exotic dancer who was into whips and things like that once wrote me to say that it was her favorite book.

**BO**: What was the most gratifying aspect of the book's reception?

**RH**: Most people get it. Most people understand what the book is about. Some people do ask, "Was she the real thing or wasn't she?" As far as I'm concerned, she was the real thing. But I wanted to have that sense of ambiguity that one always encounters when looking at saints' lives.

I once read that according to ghost hunters, when you go into a house you almost never see a ghost by looking straight at it, but you can often see it out of the corner of your eye. I think that's what happens in fiction: If you address something straight, people either accept it or reject it. But if you approach it tangentially, then they absorb it and it becomes more theirs. In the novel I wanted to leave enough space that you fill in the gaps, and it becomes much more your story than you're aware of. That's why it's distorted in time and goes back and forth a bit. There isn't a seamless narrative that lets you become a passive reader. In fact, you're creating the narrative as you go along.

In high school we read that poem by William Carlos Williams: "So much depends upon a red wheelbarrow glazed with rain water beside the white chickens." We went over and over it, and if you asked people what was going on in that little poem, you would find that they were creating all kinds of little worlds. They were firm in their belief that this was taking place in Iowa, or New Jersey, or wherever. Williams's elliptical way of talking about the world actually opens it up in a lot of ways.

**BO**: I'd like to ask about the relation of your work to film. Several of your novels have been made into films. *Isn't It Romantic?* is an homage to the filmmaker Preston Sturges, and parts of *Mariette in Ecstasy* read almost like a shooting script. Would you say that you have a particularly cinematic imagination?

**RH**: I would. When I grew up there were really only two television stations, and not a lot of content. To fill up the hours, they'd run all kinds of old films from the thirties and forties, three or four a night. I saw *Citizen Kane* for the first time when I was nine years old and was blown away by it. I bet I've seen ten times as many films as I've read novels—and I'm someone who reads a lot of novels. That's bound to govern your way of telling a story. For example, in film you often see close-ups of the lips or eyes, as opposed to in a Dickens novel, where you're seeing the whole tableau as if in a stage play, with all the characters seen full-length. Today, because of our filmic imaginations, we're much more likely to see the knuckles of somebody's hand, if that's important.

I was especially aware of Ingmar Bergman's way of telling a story when I was writing *Mariette in Ecstasy*—the way he'd just look at a clock ticking. In the opening of *The Magic Flute,* he shows close-ups of people in the audience. They aren't necessarily beautiful people, but somehow having the camera focus on them in such a loving way made them beautiful. I was trying to do that with the novel, to show that, in the same way that a camera lens lovingly receives what it's looking at, God is looking at all these aspects of life, including people who we might see as profane or gross, and accepting them as wonderful manifestations of what he created.

**BO**: Your essay "Writing as Sacrament" grew out of a talk you gave at the 1993 *Image* conference on the theme of "Silence, Cunning, and Exile: Saying the Unsayable in the Nineties." Noting the irony of the application of Stephen Dedalus's famous description of the path of the modern writer rebelling against religious (and other) constraints, you wrote that today "in a society that seems increasingly secular and post-biblical it is [the] writers and artists of faith who may feel exiled or silenced, who may feel they may say the unsayable only through cunning." You wrote that in the early nineties. Has that situation changed over the past fifteen years?

**RH**: I don't think the situation has changed. Perhaps some of my most overtly religious stuff has been received well, but I think people are still inclined to call this a post-Christian society. Whereas in the forties and fifties you'd see most movies paying homage to Catholic priests and religious life, nowadays in film you almost can't imagine a priest being treated in a good way. I recently saw a trailer for the film *In Bruges*, which opens with a hit-man shooting a priest in a confessional, and it's played for laughs. Something like that would have been unthinkable in the days of Bing Crosby.

In the 1960s, a philosopher named Anthony Flew wrote a book called *God and Philosophy*, which I read back in my Philosophy of God course in 1969. He was an atheist who mostly attacked Aquinas. Apparently, a couple of years ago, in his eighties, he decided he was a theist, or at least a deist. He reversed his position on several points. But some journalists presented him as a doddering old man who was going senile, because only a senile person could become a theist. It calls for courage to claim yourself as a religious person, to practice your religion, to go through these hardships, to be put down in the media.

**BO**: *Mariette in Ecstasy* is about a saintly person, but there's a lot of darkness and violence in the novel. In *Hitler's Niece*, you approach the topic of evil directly. What drew you to write about Hitler's inner circle?

**RH**: In *Mariette* and *Hitler's Niece*, I'm really meditating on two questions from the Spiritual Exercises: How does Christ attract followers? And how does the evil one attract followers? With *Mariette*, I'd tried to show how a woman who is in love with Jesus has to encounter difficulties in her pursuit. When I began to meditate on the second question, I thought of Hitler. I remember watching television pictures of him speaking when I was a little kid. Even if you didn't know German, you could tell from his body language how much venom he was spewing. He would work himself into a state of apoplectic rage almost instantly. I remember how scary and compelling that was. When Albert Speer saw those pictures, he said, "You have no idea what it was really like. This doesn't even capture one degree of what it was like to be in his presence." I realized that Hitler was a man who was incredibly charismatic and magnetic in the most evil way, and he had turned the world upside down, in all of its values. For him good was bad, bad was good; truth was inimical to him; hatred was something he thrived on. He really was a satanic personage, I think. I wanted to address that and show how such a personage can capture your attention and attract you and hold you. It's through blandishments, through gifts, through figuring you out, finding your points of pride and vanity. He was a master manipulator. I wanted to show that in its early stages, before he became chancellor, when he was just a rising politician. What was he doing that people found attractive, and why did they swear their allegiance to him? It was because he followed their points of hate. He made their hate his and his hate theirs.

**BO**: It takes a long time to write a novel. Did it strain you to inhabit a world so rife with evil for so long?

**RH**: When Haley Joel Osment acted in *The Sixth Sense,* he was ten or twelve years old. When he first read the script he thought it was really scary and wondered what it would be like to be on that movie set. But when he got there, he saw these people in grotesque make-up throwing Frisbees back and forth and drinking coffee, and it was just a normal workday. The same thing happens when you're writing a novel. You're imagining a scene, but you're thinking, what's the best verb to use here? It's dissociative. You're so involved behind the scenes moving things around that the horror doesn't get to you. At least it didn't for me. I didn't have any terrible dreams. My wife had terrible dreams, though.

**BO**: You sound like more of an old-fashioned craftsman than a method actor. Does that approach allow you to go deeper?

**RH**: I think the method-actor approach is probably what did in people like Fitzgerald and Hemingway. They thought you had to live the wild life in order to write about it. I'm much more in the pattern of Gustave Flaubert, who tells writers, be regular and orderly in your life, so that you can be violent and original in your work. John Irving says that sometimes when you read certain writers you can hear the ice cubes tinkling in their cocktail glasses. But you just can't live that life very long and keep producing good work.

**BO**: Most of your novels have been historical, with *Isn't it Romantic?* and *Atticus* as the exceptions. Do you think of these two as deliberate departures, as curveballs to your readership?

**RH**: Men are famous channel changers, but I'm the reverse of that. I can watch any channel and find it fascinating. I have lots of different interests. These novels are expressions of all my different interests. I am a big fan of Preston Sturges, and I thought it would be great to write a Preston Sturges kind of novel, with hopes that it would become a Preston Sturges kind of movie some day. I wrote *Isn't It Romantic?* because I thought it was good to write an entertainment in the time right after 9/11, as a reprieve for myself and for readers.

Right now I'm writing a comic film noir story. I find a lot of the things people in crime do fabulously funny, even though there's death involved. They always make so many boneheaded mistakes, and it's uproarious if you're watching from a distance. I'm not intentionally throwing a curveball. I'm just following what I'm interested in.

I want to have the freedom to write all kinds of things. I never want to be pigeonholed in any way. I might be upsetting to people, who might see me writing about saintly people and then writing about Hitler and ask, how are these of a piece? But I think they are of a piece. Fiction is a way of addressing all sides of human nature, the bright side and the dark side. They roil around in you all the time. You're always tamping down one or the other.

**BO**: Reviewers often note that your work occupies a pretty rare place, being both accessible to a wide audience and "serious." Is that something that you strive for consciously? What is your sense of audience when you write?

**RH**: I do try to be accessible and clear. I'm not at all reluctant to write, *Otto von Bismarck, chancellor of Germany*—to explain who the guy is. A friend and I always argue about this. He always thinks I'm being too obvious and I always think he's being too recondite. I think it's important to use your book as a teaching mechanism, in the same way that in the classroom I try to make clear what's going on and not put somebody down just because they haven't heard of something. But at the same time I have artistic standards I'm going for, and models or influences who I'd like to pretend would read my books with appreciation. In writing a book about Hopkins I'm aware that I probably have lots of things wrong, but I hope that Hopkins would read it and delight in it. But at the same time I want to make it available to a person who hasn't read any poems by Hopkins before, who really isn't interested in Jesuit poets.

I decided in writing *Mariette* that there was no way of explaining all of the elements of the Catholic religion, so I had to push readers in at the deep end of the pool and expect that they'd flail around and finally figure it out. As a writer, mostly you do that by showing characters in action rather than explaining things. I once wrote an essay about playing golf in bad weather, and it was bought by the *San Jose Mercury News*. One of the editors called me up and asked me to explain what a tee box was. I said that if I had to start explaining stuff like that, the story would never go. You can't write, "A tee box, a swatch of grass with a peg called a tee on which you rest the ball. . . ." It's boring. It's much better to assume people know more than they think they know.

**BO**: How does your teaching relate to your writing?

**RH**: Teaching allows you to explore things in more specific terms than you would normally. Right now I'm teaching a film noir class. I had read *The Maltese Falcon* before, but knowing that you're going to have to get up and talk about something gets you to read better. Now I'm seeing all kinds of new things, intentional things that Dashiell Hammett was doing. And that's the joy of it. It's also a way of focusing. Before, I could talk about film noir in general terms, but now that I'm teaching the class I can say, these are seven things to look for in film noir. For example, if the woman is a victim, it's not film noir. The woman always has to be in a superior position. Before, film noir was a vague, fuzzy notion to me. Doing that categorization helps you focus as a writer.

**BO**: You had a Jesuit education, and you've been teaching at a Jesuit university for over ten years now. How hopeful are you that church-related higher education is passing on a meaningful vision of "faith seeking understanding" to the next generation of students?

**RH**: Most of the Jesuit universities I know have somebody on staff who's focused on making sure the institution stays Jesuit. Some day there may be only one Jesuit there on the entire campus, but I think there's a concern with having lay colleagues who imbibe that spirit, who are Ignatian in some way. I think that's hopeful.

I became a permanent deacon in 2007, and I now witness marriages. I notice that people don't pay a lot of attention to their religion in their teens and twenties, but when they get married, they want to get married in a church, in a sacramental ceremony. Then, when they have their first child, they want to have that child baptized, and that usually brings them back to the faith. When I see students in their twenties, I know there's going to be a transformation somewhere along the line.

Sometimes they wait a long time. Norman Mailer would have had his eighty-fifth birthday tomorrow. One of his last articles was in *Playboy*, telling how he had become a Christian. I think that happens to a lot of people as they get closer to death's door. They start thinking about things. They put aside some of the rollicking things they used to do. As they become more frail, there's a greater sense of their own helplessness. And who do you look to when you're helpless? God.

**BO**: How did you come to be ordained a deacon, and what does that entail?

**RH**: I didn't foresee this when I got my master's degree. When I started writing *Mariette in Ecstasy*, it had been twenty years since I'd taken any classes in theology, so I decided I needed to catch up. On the first day of class, we went around and talked about ourselves, and these people had a theological vocabulary that intimidated me. It was totally over my head. Then I started picking up the nuances of the talk, and that was useful for the novel.

In the church, when people realize you know things, they ask you to do more. I became a lector, and a Eucharistic minister, and those things felt nourishing, and I just got more deeply involved. I'm now co-chair of the ongoing formation committee for the diocese. I also tend to be the person they call upon for weddings in mixed marriages where the couple doesn't want a mass but they want a blessing. I assist some of the Jesuits at masses on occasion, especially when they don't have time to do the homily. I do a little spiritual direction, mostly Ignatian, but often just talking and listening to what's going on in somebody's life. I don't think I'm particularly adept at spiritual direction, but people ask me, so I do it.

In the old church, the deacons were just elders, people who could be counted on, a stable force within the congregation. I think that's still the proper role for deacons. I'm not trying to confuse it with priestly functions.

I still consider writing a primary aspect of my diaconate.

**BO**: What other contemporary Catholic writers do you read?

**RH**: Tobias Wolff. Religion comes up only occasionally in his writing, but he is a practicing Catholic. Patricia Hampl, the poet and memoirist. Paul Mariani, of course. They're out there. Sometimes they're secretive. Jim Shepard considers himself a Catholic writer, but it only comes through in his fiction sporadically.

**BO**: What are you working on now?

**RH**: I've wanted to work on something about a congressman who gets in the kind of situation Gary Condit did with Chandra Levy. The congressman has had an affair with a young woman, and then she ends up missing, and his life is ruined. Gary Condit did not kill Chandra Levy, and yet he's no longer a congressman. Last I heard he was running a Baskin-Robbins ice cream store someplace. He lost everything based on innuendo. This is what the media can do.

The idea is somewhat based on Heinrich Böll's *The Lost Honor of Katharina Blum*, a novel about a woman who has a one-night stand with a guy who turns out to be a terrorist. She's arrested, interviewed by police investigators, and smeared in the tabloids. It's a novel about the media's power, and how careful we should be when we watch and read. My novel would be about a Book of Job situation, where the guy's friends turn on him and everything goes wrong, and what that means about our society.

I've outlined the initial chapters, but I don't know enough about the ending to start writing. I always have to know the ending before I get started. To tell a joke you have to know the punch line, so that you know what to include to set up the punch line. That's how I construct novels, too.

John Grisham says he spends so much time on his outlines that writing the novels becomes simple. He says eventually he gets more involved with the plot than with the characters. That's endemic to suspense novels, he thinks. When I try to write something to do with suspense, I'm much more interested in character development than plot, but I know the plot has to be there. It's the armature that everything is built on.

**BO**: The theme of exile runs through your work, whether it's the criminal "exile" of the Daltons and Jameses or the more theological understanding of exile in *Atticus, Mariette in Ecstasy*, and your new novel. Can you talk a bit about the importance of that theme for you?

**RH**: Any of us can feel as persecuted and alone as those nuns on the *Deutschland*. It could be because of an illness, the loss of a loved one, or a death sentence from cancer. Like the nuns in that shipwreck, we wonder why this is happening to us when there was so much else we could have been doing. The nuns are all young women, and they're going to work at a hospital. What could be better than that? When you look at their deaths, you think, does God want us to fail? Why does he cut people off in their prime when we need them for so many things? Almost every reader will have some life instance that's made them feel this way. We're all exiles. I even think if you could really talk to the presidential candidates, they'd say, "I never felt like I was one with the people. I've always been different."

To be an artist is to feel like an outsider or an outlaw in some way. Probably that's true of any profession, but writers and artists seem to make a special claim to that feeling of aloofness. Even as a kid I remember feeling like I was operating within a group and yet watching it from the outside at the same time. I think that's why people become writers. Most writers I know *did* fit in. They were athletes and student body presidents, yet they realized that they didn't truly belong. And you're naturally drawn to write about lives that are analogous to your own, to figures who are in the world but not of it. Mariette is as much an outlaw as Jesse James is.

To stake a claim to making a work of art is an outrageous thing. It's an exercise in vanity, pride, and ego, but also of the artistic impulse. A novel is a monologue: you're grabbing somebody by their lapels and saying, "Listen to me," which takes a certain amount of narcissism. Writing calls up all your virtues, but also some of your vices. It's a confessional experience. When you sit down to write, you're as aware of your sinfulness as you are of the nice things you've done for people, and in some ways you relish those sins because you can put them into your characters. You write about what you could have become, if not for some change of trajectory. You write about people who are susceptible to the same things you are. Outlaws and exiles allow you to exaggerate what you find that's negative in yourself.

**BO**: You've written about the idea of writing as sacrament. How has your thinking on that developed?

**RH**: I go back to the old idea that a sacrament is a visible sign of an invisible grace. I liken writing to sacrament in that way. Writing witnesses to something that's happened to you, or to some power that's moving through you. In writing, you're trying to communicate what's been going on in you spiritually and make it somehow tangible to others. You're trying to give it life. And that's what the sacraments are intended to do. They're symbols of something that God is actually doing to us. We believe that the Eucharist is the whole presence of God, but the ceremony surrounding the Eucharist is also a symbol of the life of Christ: his birth, his call for repentance, his baptism, and his sacrifice on the table. Sacraments all function as ways of telling stories about God's relationship to us. And that's what I think writing is doing as well.

# THE NOVEL AS BIOGRAPHY
## An Interview with Michael Lackey

**Michael Lackey**: Let me begin by telling you about the nature of this project. I'm trying to figure out why starting in the 1980s so many prominent writers began to author biographical novels. I'm also trying to define the nature of this genre of fiction. Can you start by explaining why you have written novels about Gerard Manley Hopkins and Hitler's niece?

**Ron Hansen**: I'm always looking for lively stories to tell and am not much interested in writing about myself. And I read a lot of history and biography and often find myself so captivated by the narratives that I begin seeing the unfolding events as cinematic scenes. There's a "Wow!" factor that makes me wonder why nobody else has written the story with all its possibilities as fiction. I was especially struck by Geli Raubal, Hitler's niece, a little-known girl in the Weimar Republic. But Hitler always said that she was the only woman he ever loved or would ever consider marrying. After her death, he had all-night vigils before her portrait each Christmas Eve. Everybody knows that Hitler had a thanatos complex in that he was only really interested in people after they were dead. Some say it was partly because of the trauma he experienced in watching his mother die. Eva Braun only excited him after she attempted suicide, and they both successfully completed the act after their wedding in the *führer* bunker. In *Hitler's Niece*, I saw myself as a prosecuting attorney building a case to demonstrate that Hitler either had murdered Geli or had ordered her done away with. And I was fascinated that so many historians simply accepted the fact that she had killed herself with her uncle's pistol when there was no evidence that she was suicidal. She was even in the midst of writing a hopeful letter to a girlfriend in Vienna. But Geli knew too much; she was dangerous. Had she left Adolf's purview and control she might have given away secrets that would have destroyed his political career. In the novel I felt I was developing my case for a jury of readers.

**ML**: I suspect that you had a different orientation and approach in your first biographical novel, *Desperadoes*.

**RH**: I happened upon *The Dalton Gang*, a biographical study by Harold Preece, and immediately saw it as a fascinating story. Emmett Dalton was the sole survivor of the gang's failed attempt to rob two banks simultaneously in their hometown of Coffeyville, Kansas. That was in 1892 and in some ways represented the end of the Wild West. He did time in prison, married his childhood sweetheart, lived into the late 1930s as a tee-totaling real estate broker and building contractor in Los Angeles, and saw his own memoir, *When the Daltons Rode*, turned into a movie. When, in old age, he returned to Coffeyville, he was celebrated by the very defenders who'd killed his brothers. *Desperadoes* is about wild youths and reckless ambition and the transition from the Old West to the new.

**ML**: And you followed that with another biographical novel, *The Assassination of Jesse James by the Coward Robert Ford*.

**RH**: William Kittredge read *Desperadoes* and asked me to write a short story about the Old West for a special issue of *TriQuarterly*. Because I had written about the Dalton Gang, who'd strived to imitate the misdeeds of the James-Younger Gang, I ended up knowing an awful lot about Jesse James. It seemed to me nobody had ever told the full and accurate story of how and why Bob Ford killed Jesse James, so I began writing that as a short story. After about thirty pages, I realized I had just scratched the surface, so I apologized to Bill Kittredge but told him I thought I'd found my next novel.

**ML**: Did you have any models for doing this kind of fiction?

**RH**: Not novels, but Shakespeare's plays. So many of them were biographical. He took the rough facts of history but then supplied further context, invented romance and drama, and presented it all in wonderfully poetic dialogue. But the characters, incidents, and rough shape of his plays would have been very familiar to his initial audiences. His plays were a way of giving new and enriched life to recognizable figures while also giving his imagination room to play with his fictional interpretation of events.

**ML**: Did you ever read Styron's *Confessions of Nat Turner?*

**RH**: Yes I did.

**ML**: Do you see that as a successful biographical novel?

**RH**: I read it, but I didn't like it as much as others have.

**ML**: Why?

**RH**: I thought it was overwrought and I didn't believe that this was the real Nat Turner.

**ML**: That was Russell Banks's critique. He thought it was a failed novel because it didn't accurately reflect who Turner probably was.

**RH**: I agree. However, Styron's novel provided the inspiration and freedom to write a biographical novel back in the late 70s. The same thing with E.L. Doctorow's *Ragtime.* Doctorow took real characters, such as Harry Houdini and J. P. Morgan put them in actual historical situations, but through irony, comedy, and the sheer zest of his writing made nineteenth-century America seem fabulous in both senses of the word. Earlier Doctorow had written the Western *Welcome to Hard Times,* with that and *Ragtime* I felt I was given permission to write biographical novels about the Old West. And that led to later examples.

**ML**: Let me turn to *Exiles,* which is your biographical novel about Hopkins. Hopkins was a Catholic priest and a first-rate poet. What can you communicate about Hopkins through the biographical novel that you couldn't through a traditional biography or scholarly study?

**RH**: In the novel I was trying to explain the origins of inspiration and the process of poetry writing for readers who don't know very much about the craft, and to deal with our conceptions of evil, theodicy, and failure. I was educated by the Jesuits and still have good friends in the Society of Jesus, so I felt I knew something of Gerard's religious yearnings, and I could analogize a poet's life from my experiences as a prose writer. I knew the exaltations and frustrations of teaching, I thought I had a good handle on his bipolar personality, and I was wild about his poems. But unlike a historian or biographer I could speculate and make educated guesses about Fr. Hopkins and his rather tortured but ultimately successful career as a poet and priest. With his biographer, my old friend Paul Mariani, I visited Hopkins's theologate of St. Beuno's in Wales so I could give readers an accurate description of the room he slept in, the hallways he walked, the faces of sheep chewing grass in the meadow. Those are the things historians have to overlook but that have meaning for readers. The accumulation of details enables readers to share the experiences of the fictional characters and situations.

**ML**: Can you briefly make some distinctions between your earlier biographical novels and your later ones, such as *Hitler's Niece* and *Exiles*? You do something very different with each one of them and I am starting to notice that there are subgenres of the biographical novel. For instance, Zora Neale Hurston, Anita Diamant, and Rebecca Kanner have done biographical novels based on the Bible. Would you say that your novels are in different sub-genres?

**RH**: There is a difference based on the amount of available information, which enables some to have more fidelity to the historical record. There was not much known about the Dalton gang. I knew about their robberies and how they died, and I knew what they looked like because there were photographs available. But almost none of their dialogue was available. Emmett Dalton's memoir was playing fast and loose with the truth, and the journalism of the day was full of misrepresentations and hyperbole. So my writing and invention could be more pliable.

As for Jesse James and Robert Ford, there was greater fame. A lot more was known about them and I carefully researched them. I visited the places they lived, stood inside the room where Jesse was killed, read the same *Kansas City Star* he would have been reading.

Eighty-nine books had been written about Gerard Manley Hopkins when *Exiles* was published so I knew an awful lot about him, but very little about the nuns who died in the shipwreck of the *Deutschland*, and half the book is about them. There seemed to me different obligations in terms of fidelity to the truth for each of those novels, but I'm not sure that constitutes a subgenre. Some biographical novelists have a very elastic view of the truth, and some are much more faithful. The fiction writers I really admire, like my friend Jim Shepard, are always very scrupulous about the facts. But what a novelist is expected to provide are things that are not recorded by history: private moments, intimate conversations, gestures, weather, and smell of the food. But that's what gives vitality to long-over-with events.

**ML:** The literary critic Georg Lukács condemned the biographical novel in his work *The Historical Novel* and he did so because he believed it necessarily distorts and misrepresents history. In *Exiles*, you engage history by mentioning the laws that led to the persecution of Catholics in Germany, England, and Ireland, but you focus mainly on the ways those anti-Catholic laws destroy the lives of people such as Hopkins and the five nuns he wrote about in his poem "The Wreck of the Deutschland." Can you talk about the role the biographical novel plays in accessing and picturing a particular dimension of history?

**RH:** But Lukács admired the historical realism in Balzac and Tolstoy and Sir Walter Scott, so we're not that far apart. I think the biographical novel provides much-needed context for historical events and functions like those connect-the-dots pictures in which you only see the hidden face or object after you have drawn all the lines. Historians usually focus on a few of those dots, generally the economic or political.

But other cultural, physical, or metaphysical dots really hit people where they live. For instance, when I was writing about Jesse James hiding out in St. Joseph, Missouri the daily front page news in the *Kansas City Star* was about Charles Guiteau, who'd been convicted of assassinating President James A. Garfield and was about to be executed. Wouldn't the idea of assassination of a public figure and the fame that followed be very influential to Bob Ford? Yet earlier historians and biographers never brought it up because it wouldn't have seemed pertinent given the shape and expectations for their books.

The biographical novelist tells the truth about the events but also gives the reader a sense of what the glimpsed human beings must have been like and how they were nudged and determined by the circumstances around them. Jesse James was killed not on a Saturday night as song and legend has it, but on the Monday morning of Holy Week, and on the day after Palm Sunday when there probably was a sermon on the crucifixion of Jesus that would come with Good Friday. Some historians would not find that important to include, but it would have been part of the collective unconscious of the time. The effect that had on Southern sympathizers was monumental as they perhaps unwittingly linked Jesse's death with the crucifixion of Jesus, linked the Missouri governor with Pontius Pilate, and envisioned Bob Ford as a latter-day Judas.

**ML**: Do you think the limitation with historians is their method of analysis? Or, do you think that there is something in the skillset of the novelists that enables them to access something about history, character, and motivation that is significantly different from historians?

**RH**: I think historians are interested in the consequences or *doings* of a character and novelists are interested in the being, the motivations. What governs their psychology? What are the existential facts of their life? Are they resentful? Hungry? Do they have ailments? Historians have a thesis or argument they buttress with established facts. Novelists have similar opinions but they personify them and act them out. It's precisely how debate and drama differ.

**ML**: In the author's note to *Hitler's Niece* you describe your novel as a work of fiction that is based on fact, but you make an important qualification: "most consequential moments of any person's life go un-glimpsed by either historians or journalists, and those intimate moments are where fiction finds its force and interest." Therefore, you claim that you "felt free to invent in those instances, but always in the spirit of likelihood and fidelity to the record." Can you talk about your strategies and techniques for representing one of those consequential moments in your Hopkins novel?

**RH**: When Hopkins first starts writing the poem "The Wreck of the Deutschland" he shows it to one of his friends—a fellow scholastic who is also studying theology in Wales—and Hopkins at once wants to show off the new meter in his poetry. Hopkins says he doubts that an editor will ever publish the poem, or as he said in a letter, "The journals will think it barbarous." And his classmate asks, "Why write it, then?" And Hopkins replies in puzzlement, "Why pray?" As far as I know Hopkins never likened his poetry to prayer; that's a self-revelation concerning my feelings about writing fiction that I'm guessing Gerard would agree with. There are moments of inspiration in fiction writing, moments where you feel you are in a waking dream that you're not fully responsible for. And the feeling is very similar to prayer, when you make yourself vulnerable, permeable, an instrument of God's will. In each case you hope that there is some kind of consequence that is useful to yourself and to others.

**ML**: But why should we trust your depiction of such a consequential moment?

**RH**: Well, that's for readers to judge. The novel will be a success if it persuades the reader to say: "Oh yeah, it must have happened that way." Yet there's also a dichotomy. Readers, for example, might look at a dinner table conversation among the five nuns in *Exiles* and realize that it is funnier or more modern than it probably could have been, and even while they realize that the author is putting words in the five women's mouths they would be recognizing the usefulness and enjoyment of getting a sense of five separate personalities. And as I say in the note to *Exiles*, we know so little about these women. I looked into biographies of nineteenth-century European foundresses with the objective of recognizing and capturing the stirrings that motivate a girl to go into religious life. So there was a factual basis for my characterizations that I hoped would provide a convincing verisimilitude to my recreated people. You try to persuade readers of the logic and fidelity of your truth.

**ML**: In *Exiles* you give readers individual sections about each nun's background. When reading, I was wondering: are these your representations of the nuns? Or, are they supposed to be your Hopkins's representations as he is doing research in preparation for writing the poem?

**RH**: No, it's all mine. He never even mentions the names of the nuns in "The Wreck of the Deutschland." At most you get him describing Sister Barbara Hültenschmidt as "a lioness," "a prophetess," and "a tall one." He just knows those five sisters died.

**ML**: Did he do much research?

**RH**: No, there was almost nothing available to him then. The newspaper accounts that he would have had access to were just the *London Times* and even then he was in the midst of his theological studies and had very little opportunity to do further research. Once he asked his mother to send him information, and she sent him the wrong newspaper clipping. In his exasperation he just worked with his own experiences of conversion, what he spottily knew about the shipwreck, and with general principles of

HOTLY IN PURSUIT OF THE REAL

Catholic teaching, particularly as they have to do with human suffering. I invented the scene where Gerard goes to the cemetery and finds their names on the headstone. As far as I know he never did that, though the cemetery was close to his boyhood home.

**ML:** There's an author's note in both *Hitler's Niece* and *Exiles* and they both start with the same sentence: "This is a work of fiction based on fact." However, there is a major discrepancy in the length of the two notes. In the 1999 novel about Hitler's niece the note is almost three pages long, while in the 2008 novel about Hopkins the note is a short paragraph that is less than a page long. Can you explain why there is such a difference in the length of these two notes?

**RH:** The difference in *Exiles* is that the notation is divided into two parts. There's the first part, an Author's Note about how I went about creating the novel, and then at the end there is "A Note on My Sources." *Hitler's Niece* puts those explanations, or justifications, together in the same note.

**ML:** But in *Hitler's Niece* you have about five paragraphs defending your approach and clarifying your method, whereas in *Exiles* there is only one short paragraph.

**RH:** I wonder if that's because by 2008 there seemed to be more of an acceptance of the biographical novel. I remember that when *Hitler's Niece* was published in 1999 an Australian review called such a handling of historical characters a "newfangled" idea. I heard none of that with *Exiles*. And of course fictional representations of real lives is actually a very old idea. Even Homer's *Iliad* is based on real people.

**ML:** But a lot of those works changed the characters' names. For instance, in *All the King's Men* Robert Penn Warren changes Huey Long's name to Willie Stark. Why don't contemporary novelists do this as much anymore?

**RH:** Perhaps it's because libel laws have loosened up. You have to justify that your privacy has been invaded or you have actually been wounded by someone's account. Early on novelists hid behind the guise of the *roman à clef* so they'd have more freedom with the basic material. But perhaps they noticed that biographical films were depicting real people with impunity and decided if movies could get away with it, fiction could get away with it, too. But once you use a real person's name, you have to be faithful to the events and what he or she was like unless your characterization is so outlandish—as in Robert Coover's portrayal of Richard Nixon in *The Public Burning*—that the public would recognize it as a cartoon.

**ML:** Ralph Ellison argues that the moment you become historically specific you limit your character's possibility for having universal significance. For instance, he was very critical of William Styron for naming the character Nat Turner. Ellison adopted this view because he wants to portray more universal meanings. For instance, in *Invisible Man* he refers to the Brotherhood, which clearly represents the Communist Party. But he never explicitly says that the Brotherhood is the Communist Party. The reason why is he wanted it to be not just the Communist Party but any kind of political organization. Calling it the Brotherhood gives him more freedom to signify in a universal way, whereas the moment you become historically specific you lose that kind of universalizing capacity. Would you agree with that?

**RH:** I disagree totally. We work by analogy. If I talk about a real person and real events, the reader can still make the connection to something that is going on now. One of my problems with *Invisible Man*, which I've taught many times, is that the book is *too* allegorical. I knew Ellison was referring to the Communist Party, even my dullest students did, and it didn't enlarge the narrative at all to think of the Brotherhood in a more vague and general way.

**ML:** Biographical novelists consistently invent scenes in order to communicate something about a biographical figure or an historical event. For instance in *Hitler's Niece* you skillfully build up to the scene when Geli meets the Catholic priest Rupert Mayer for the second time. This scene resonates powerfully. However you mention in your author's note that you have no idea whether Geli met Rupert Mayer. Why include this scene? And what does it communicate to the reader about Geli's situation? Finally, what does this fictional scene communicate about the history of Nazi Germany?

**RH:** Fr. Rupert Mayer was one of the first to discover how dangerous Hitler was. He spied on many of Hitler's early speeches, recorded what was going on, and warned his congregation about him. Geli Raubal was Catholic and probably still regularly went to Masses despite her uncle's antagonism to any religion not centered on himself. He and Geli were living in a posh Munich apartment not far from St. Michael's Parish where the Jesuit priest was assigned, so it's entirely likely that she could have happened into a Mass where he preached. She was certainly in need of somebody outside of Hitler's Nazi circle to talk to as she gradually came to realize what the uncle she formerly adored was really like. And that set in motion her ultimate fate.

**ML:** Do you think that biographical novelists can access certain kinds of truths, historical truths if you will, that can expand the borders of knowledge in ways that other intellectual professionals cannot? And why should we trust the findings of biographical novelists?

**RH:** Our first chore is to make history accessible. There are people who read biographical novels who would never dream of reading straight biography. And as I said, we supply the flavor and context of the times. A friend of mine, when reading *Desperadoes* in our Stanford workshop, said whenever his telephone rang he had to shake himself out of the nineteenth century to answer it. Ideally that is what you want to force readers to do with historical or biographical fiction. I was at an American history convention, and the historians were debating these very issues, noting there was a fierce division within the history camp as some remained obedient to the rigid rules of evidence while others sought to become more popular and more compelling by adopting the practices of fiction writers.

**ML:** The compelling nature of fiction to illuminate history?

**RH:** Yes.

**ML:** In 1968 there was a famous debate on this topic. The historian C. Vann Woodward moderated a round-table conversation with Ralph Ellison, Robert Penn Warren, and William Styron. He started by making a distinction between history and fiction. But both Ellison and Warren insisted that history is fiction. Their claim goes like this: historians think that they are doing something that is nonfiction but because they frame the material in a particular way and because the information is mediated through a specific consciousness, it is naïve for historians to think that they stand above or outside fiction. Would you agree with that?

**RH:** Oh totally. I point out to my classes that fiction comes from the past participle of the Latin *fingere*, which means to shape or to mold. History is already shaped by the very selection of the material that historians choose to write about. As soon as they have a focus, they also have an agenda. They ignore some things and highlight others. I have a world respect for historians and honor their important efforts, but I think most would agree that they shape information in order to make their points. Otherwise they would end up with a profuse and unwieldy mess.

**ML:** Do you think that this postmodern breakdown of the distinction between fact and fiction has contributed significantly to the rise of the biographical novel?

**RH:** Postmodernism certainly makes people feel freer to invent and distort. But the finest biographical novelists still feel that they have to obey certain rules, that there are boundaries. Take, for instance, Jay Parini's *The Last Station*. Relying on authentic historical incidents, Jay felt free to invent scenes and conversations but within the realm of likelihood. And because of that his novel is persuasive and seemingly true to Tolstoy's life.

**ML:** So when you call your work a novel, you are implicitly saying that you have the freedom to take more liberties than an historian. But when you call a work history, or a memoir, or a biography, you have less freedom. Can you specify the kind of freedoms you can take as a novelist but that you cannot take as an historian?

**RH:** When I was working on *Hitler's Niece*, my wife and I stopped off at an Austrian inn for dinner and ate at a lakeside picnic table. At another table were four Austrian men with two bawdy women who could only have been prostitutes. They seemed to have been having a wild old weekend. When I imagined Hitler and Geli vacationing on a similar lake in 1930, I introduced those Austrians into the surroundings to make visual the kind of renegade cultural values of the time.

**ML:** So you take an episode from the contemporary world and extract from it a mentality or an aura that you then incorporate into your novel.

**RH:** That's right, because you are trying to capture the sensuality of an event. And you have to do that with visual stimuli or sounds or tastes that the historian is denied. But once you start playing with such things, incorporating too much from another world, the narrative can become confused and pointless.

**ML**: So can you specify what liberty you cannot take?

**RH**: When I was adapting *Desperadoes* for film, there was a scene in which the Dalton Gang rides into Coffeyville and gets wiped out while trying to hold up two banks at the same time. A movie producer, thinking of box office, asked, "Why do we have to have them die? Why couldn't they live through it?" Well, I'd heard that the producer of Robert Altman's classic Western *McCabe & Mrs. Miller* had been upset in a similar way when his star Warren Beatty was killed in the ending so I realized that our producer, like him, was thinking it was too much of a bummer for audiences to see their idols die on screen.

But I thought that alteration would have been such a significant violation of fact that I would have found it impossible to script in that way. The Dalton family was large but I neglected those who were not criminals. I have no problem with that. But shifting too far from the history seems wrong to me, and an insult to the memory of the people who are my focus. Just as poets obey the meter and rhyme of their form, I feel constrained to get across what must have happened and what the protagonists actually did. When Jesse James is shot in the back of the head, his wife rushed in from the kitchen and saw Bob Ford standing there in the gun smoke, and as she knelt to her husband she screamed, "Bob, have you done this?" He said, "The gun went off accidentally," and she replied, "Yes, accidentally on purpose." Most journals of the period carried that contemporary-sounding account, but it probably seemed like an anachronistic off-note in my novel. Yet I felt I could not get rid of it and was stuck with having to make the sentences work because they were on record.

**ML**: Could we say that you have two separate approaches as a biographical novelist? On the one hand, your job is to make a story realistic and enjoyable so that it is accessible for contemporary readers. On the other hand, your job is to dig into the archives and the logic of character and narrative in order to get to a more accurate assessment of what happened historically. You do this in order to give us a more realistic and accurate picture of history. Is that correct?

**RH**: Exactly. You approach these things with a sense of wonder. How is it possible that this event happened in this way? Why haven't other people talked about it? You've come to a conclusion yourself and then you go back and try to connect the prompts and reactions. And you ask yourself: in my experience of humanity, do people act this way? If they don't, then I know there's something wrong with the narrative. You use the history to justify each step you take, but you also use your own sense of psychology and human nature to make all those things authoritative. If one element doesn't add up to another, then you know you're on the wrong track.

**ML**: Why did you center *Hitler's Niece* within the consciousness of Geli? And what could you communicate about history through this focus on the relationship between Hitler and Geli?

**RH**: Geli was my stand-in for Germany, illustrating how Hitler was able to woo an entire nation by telling the people what they wanted to hear, offering blandishments and scapegoats, exciting some of their worst impulses, promising revenge for injuries, all while seeming an honorable leader. And Geli was an intimate who was at first captivated by and in love with Hitler. But she gradually came to understand his satanic nature. Likewise, but only after the war, Germany finally became fully aware of his evil and perversity and even now succeeding generations feel the shame of their forebears for having followed him. Had the Germans only known what Geli tragically knew, Hitler could not have run against von Hindenburg in the 1932 presidential elections, nor been appointed Chancellor by von Hindenburg a year later. Geli became for me a personification of the Germany that did not know what they were getting in Adolf and of those who correctly read the signs of the times and fled.

**ML**: To conclude, can you tell me other biographical novels that you consider outstanding? And can you explain why you consider them outstanding?

**RH**: Along with those novels I've already mentioned there are those of Julia Alvarez, *In the Time of the Butterflies*, about the vibrant, valiant Mirabal sisters and their challenge to Trujillo's dictatorship, and *Blonde* by Joyce Carol Oates, a novel I recommended for the National Book Award because of its sad, haunting, evocative representation of the life of Marilyn Monroe. Raymond Carver has a surprising and lovely last story, "Errand," about the final days of Anton Chekov. My favorite book by Norman Mailer is his "true life novel" *The Executioner's Song*, an overwhelming and perfectly-pitched account in both "Western" and "Eastern" voices of the crimes, court trials, and final execution in Utah of Gary Gilmore. My friend Jim Shepard's novel *Nosferatu* is a stunning, sympathetic fictional biography of F. W. Murnau, which captures the life of the German film director by glimpsing the man in various crises of development. Happily there are many biographical novels out there, and more are surely coming as fiction writers recognize the genre's fascination and power.

III

# SEPARATING TRUTH FROM LEGEND

## Writing *The Assassination of Jesse James by the Coward Robert Ford*

My first published novel was *Desperadoes*, a fiction informed by fact. In it I presented the history of the notorious Dalton Gang—three brothers and assorted miscreants who supplemented their miserable paychecks as lawmen in what was not yet Oklahoma by exacting tolls on pioneers, selling liquor to Indians, and then cattle and horse rustling, a hanging offense. Warrants for their arrest confirmed them as criminals, and they soon were imitating the earlier James-Younger Gang with a daring series of train robberies and bank holdups until October 1892, when their leader, Bob Dalton, decided to try to outdo Jesse James by robbing two banks at the same time in their hometown of Coffeyville, Kansas. The citizens there successfully defended their institutions, just as those in Northfield, Minnesota, had done against the James-Younger Gang, and four of the five outlaws were killed in the gun battle. Emmett Dalton, the sole survivor, served 14 years in a Kansas penitentiary before his release, at age 35, and he illustrated his rehabilitation by marrying his childhood sweetheart and moving to Los Angeles, where he was an evangelist against what he called "the evils of outlawry" and became, as he puts it in the novel, "a real-estate broker, a building contractor, a scriptwriter for Western movies; a church man, a Rotarian, a member of Moose Lodge 29."

Emmett's lout of a father often boasted that he'd once sold horses to the infamous James Gang, and the celebrity of Jesse James after his death had so much to do with the trajectory of the Daltons from honored marshals to murderous thieves that I became an expert in the James Gang while researching the Daltons. So when Bill Kittridge invited me to submit something for a special issue on the Old West he was editing for *Triquarterly*, I told him I would try a short historical fiction on how Jesse James was killed. Thirty pages into it, I told Bill I could not finish the story by deadline but thought I had a novel in the works.

Along the Missouri River north of Omaha, there was a wilderness park with a forbiddingly steep slope called "Devil's Slide" and near it, a great dirt cave that was rumored to have been a hideout for the James Gang at one time. We'd sit in that cave as boys and just imagine for a while. My grandfather would have been thirteen and handling chores on a farm in Iowa when Jesse James was killed in 1882, so it's entirely possible that as a little boy he did indeed once find the James Gang genially watering their horses at his family's stable trough. The haggard men spoke kindly to him, he claimed, and then, hearing hooves on the road, hurriedly galloped away.

Until I began researching *Desperadoes*, my sole information on Jesse James was dependent either on hand-me-down legend or on some of the thirty or more movie portrayals of him. His own son, Jesse Jr., and Tyrone Power, Roy Rogers, Audie Murphy, Robert Wagner, Robert Duvall, Kris Kristofferson, James Keach, Rob Lowe, and Colin Farrell are just some of the actors who have portrayed Jesse James over the years. Often the outlaw was presented as a Robin Hood who stole from the rich to give to the poor, or as a good and honorable man forced into crime by an unforgiving Union Army, ruthless and carnivorous railroads and banks, or the Pinkerton Detective Agency, a forerunner of the Secret Service and the FBI. And when Robert Ford was introduced at all it was usually late in the film, as a sly, slinking, serpentine traitor, or as the song has it, "that dirty little coward that shot Mr. Howard" and "laid poor Jesse in his grave."

Such a pat formula may have been fine for old-fashioned movies with their coloring book depictions of heroes and villains, but intensive research convinced me that Jesse James was a fascinating, emotionally complex, and frequently charming man who could also be a cold-blooded psychopath, and Robert Ford was scheming, yes, but his assassination of his friend was in many ways an act of self-defense, and he'd been given pressure and license to do it by none other than Thomas Crittenden, the governor of Missouri.

Even in insignificant details, earlier books and movies got the facts wrong. Jesse was shot on a Monday morning, yet because of Billy Ga-shade's enduring but erring song, the shooting was generally located on a Saturday night. Though Jesse's last words were "That picture's awful dusty," editorial cartoons featured him adjusting a needlepoint of "Home Sweet Home," and other framed images in the movies generally avoided what the picture actually was: a watercolor of the owner's favorite race-horse, Skyrocket. "Three children, they were brave," the song has it. Jesse and Zee had two little children, a boy and a girl, and neither knew their father's real name or what he did for a living, and their bravery was neces-sary only because of the misery and near destitution they were subjected to after their father's death.

But it was the controversial Bob Ford who intrigued me as much as the murderer he murdered, for he seemed not only misrepresented by his-tory, but motivated by the tendencies of arrogance, envy, greed, idolatry, and self-aggrandizement of which Shakespearean tragedies are made. On the evening of my 33rd birthday celebration, John Chapman killed John Lennon, the Beatle he deeply admired; and four months later John Hinck-ley tried to assassinate President Ronald Reagan, permanently disabling his press secretary and wounding the president and two others, all in order to weirdly impress the actress Jodie Foster. There was a good deal about past assassination attempts in the media that year, and I was drawn to the old newspaper coverage of the trial and execution of Charles Guiteau, a mentally disordered journalist and scoundrel lawyer who, because he had campaigned fitfully for Republican President James Garfield, felt he was owed an ambassadorship to Vienna or Paris, and when his crazy entreaties were ignored, shot him. All historical novels in some way interpret and comment on the years in which they were written.

At the same time that Charles Guiteau was collecting hundreds of pages of press attention for his oddities, a fame that most respectable Americans are denied, Bob Ford was plotting the capture of Jesse James with government officials who promised a reward equivalent now to more than a million dollars and, if he was forced to kill the outlaw, full exon-eration and pardon. With the grave possibility that Jesse, in his paranoia, hoped to kill Bob and his brother Charley whenever he found the likeliest opportunity, there must have seemed little downside to what the Fords decided to risk.

Often readers of such a novel ask me, "How much of this is true?" It's a reasonable question, since frequent malpractice has made the historical novel a suspect genre. My rules are fairly simple: honesty and fidelity throughout, meaning no hard facts, however inconvenient, may be dismissed and no crucial scenes, however wished for, may be turned to ends that may be more pleasing to a contemporary audience. In other words, I do not budge from the truth as I know it and I firmly root the novel in the 19th century in spite of 20th-century perceptions of what can and should be done or said. I relied primarily on period newspaper accounts, secondarily on histories, and not at all on the recollections of the descendants of family and eyewitnesses since those "memories" are the most tinged by flattering interpretation.

I have been asked why there is no exit wound in the front of his head if Jesse was shot by a revolver just behind his ear. My answer simply is that there was no exit wound because the bullet was still inside his skull— whether that is a fault of the gunpowder in the cartridge is unknown to me and did not particularly trouble the journalists at the time who noted the bullet's extraction.

I have been asked about the claim that Charles Bigelow, rather than Jesse James, was killed on April 3, 1882, and whether J. Frank Dalton, who claimed to be Jesse and thus was 103 years old when he died, was the real thing. Looking at the last item first, J. Frank Dalton was not the man's real name but one taken up in middle age on his first inclination to pretend to be Bob Dalton's older brother Franklin, and J. Frank had almost no resemblance to photographs of Jesse; he also later claimed an impossible relationship with Howard Hughes, and he seems to have been one of the unknown heroes of World War I. A fraud, in other words, but a fascinating one.

Recent medical examinations have proved the DNA of the remains in the Kearney, Missouri, grave of Jesse Woodson James in fact match the DNA in samples of other items known to have belonged to him. Cranks who still believe otherwise are not worth the argument. But even before such tests were available, the Charles Bigelow conspiracy theory made no sense. Were the funeral of Jesse James a fake, it would mean Zee James and Jesse's mother, Zerelda, were the finest actresses of the century, and Jesse, the famously loyal family man, was content to witness his wife and children living in abject poverty until Zee's premature death. Also, the assassinated corpse photographed and forensically examined in St. Joseph, Missouri, in 1882 contained every injury, physical characteristic, and dental repair of the famous outlaw.

Those injuries are much in evidence on actor Brad Pitt in the Warner Bros. film adaptation of my novel. Having grown up in Missouri, Brad was familiar with the glamorous but false representations of Jesse James and, like me, was intrigued far more by a historically accurate, psychologically acute, warts-and-all presentation of this shrewd, spellbinding, and improbably durable celebrity.

Andrew Dominik, the New Zealand director and screenwriter of our film chanced upon my novel in a used bookstore in Melbourne, and when, after the success of his stunning first film, *Chopper*, Andrew was contacted by Brad about the possibility of working together on a project for Pitt's Plan B production company, Andrew suggested *The Assassination of Jesse James by the Coward Robert Ford*. Brad loved it, including its title which he insisted Warner Bros. could not change. Within months, Andrew produced a wonderful script that is completely faithful to the novel, and on Aug. 29, 2005, principal photography began, with Casey Affleck as Bob Ford, Sam Rockwell as his brother Charley, Mary Louise Parker as Jesse's wife, Sam Shepard as Frank James, Jeremy Renner as Wood Hite, and a host of other interesting and persuasive actors playing supporting roles.

Alberta, Canada's woodlands and prairies, the mountains near Banff, and the old-town streets of Winnipeg provide settings that look far more like 1880s Missouri, eastern cities, and Bob Ford's final home in Creede, Colorado, than the authentic locations do today. Walking through the sets, I marveled at the details, with "Thomas Howard's" house at 1318 Lafayette Street in St. Joseph reconstructed exactly according to the architectural blueprint of the original building and furnished with real antiques from the period. I had a job as an extra one Wednesday afternoon—I played, without flourish, a journalist—and was costumed in some long dead man's actual 19th-century frock coat, stiffly-collared shirt, and carefully brushed black bowler hat.

The honor that the whole production—cast, crew, and studio—paid to this fragment of America's history was gratifying to the author, of course, but more importantly it was doing justice to the named and the nameless who lived in the turbulence and violence of the post-Civil War Reconstruction, and against all odds, settled a disorderly frontier.

# HOPKINS AND "THE WRECK OF THE DEUTSCHLAND"

## Writing *Exiles*

WHEN OXFORD GRADUATE GERARD MANLEY HOPKINS ENTERED THE Society of Jesus in 1868, the religious order was still open to persecution in England and was being evicted from Spain. Two years later, the Jesuit curia was expelled from Rome as the papal states were annexed by King Victor Emanuel II. In northern Europe, Chancellor Otto von Bismarck orchestrated the unification of Prussia, Bavaria, Saxony, Württemberg, and twenty other states into the Second Reich of Germany, and originated a *Kulturkampf*, or cultural struggle, that was intended to quash the political power of the country's Catholic minority, which Bismarck loathed for being more loyal to the papacy than the Reich.

Hopkins was a Jesuit scholastic in philosophy studies at Stonyhurst in 1872 when the Reichstag gave the government license to ostracize the Society of Jesus, and the first contingent of exiled German Jesuits arrived in England. Within the year their Rhineland Theologate was relocated to a village between Manchester and Liverpool, and several of their professors ended up teaching Hopkins at the Saint Beuno's Theologate in Wales.

In May 1873, Culture Minister Adalbert Falk instituted laws giving the Reich control of Catholic education, making civil marriages obligatory, and ending all financial aid to the Catholic Church while continuing it for Protestant institutions. And in 1875 a series of "May Laws" were decreed, excluding from the territories of the Prussian state all Catholic religious orders not involved in the needed job of nursing, and consigning each congregation's properties to the management of a board of trustees selected by the government.

So it was that five nuns from the order entitled Sisters of Saint Francis, Daughters of the Sacred Hearts of Jesus and Mary, left their convent in Salzkotten, Germany for nursing jobs in a Catholic hospital south of Saint Louis, Missouri. The five were Sister Barbara Hültenschmidt, aged thirty-two, Sister Norberta Reinkober, thirty, Sister Henrica Fassbender, twenty-eight, Sister Brigitta Dammhorst, twenty-seven, and Sister Aurea Badziura, twenty-three. The journey from the port of Bremen to London and then across the Atlantic Ocean was expected to take thirteen days.

"Wrecks and Casualties" was a regular department in each issue of *The Times* of London and among the Victorians there was a general fascination with tales of great tragedies at sea. But more than that, Hopkins's father was the author of *A Handbook of Average* and *A Manual of Marine Insurance,* both standard reference books for negotiating, averaging, and adjusting the liabilities to insurance underwriters of cargo losses and shipwrecks, so Hopkins grew up in a world wet with marine accidents and was especially attentive to them.

Sixteen shipwrecks were recorded in *The Times* on Wednesday, December 8th, 1875, and among them was the first news of the *Deutschland,* a transatlantic steamer that left Bremen on Saturday, the 4th, steering toward America. But it ran aground off the east coast of England on an undersea island of sand that was called the Kentish Knock. Though it did not sink, the *Deutschland* became a kind of reef that the icy North Sea crashed over throughout the night of December 6th. By the time the weather calmed and a rescue came on the late morning of the 7th, more than sixty passengers and crew had been snatched overboard by the great tonnage of waves or overcome by hypothermia in the ship's sail shrouds or drowned in the flooded saloon below the weather deck.

But what caught Hopkins's attention was the notice that among those who'd lost their lives were five Franciscan nuns who were exiled from their country because of the Falk Laws. Especially important to him was a Saturday notice in *The Times* that reported: "Five German nuns, whose bodies are now in the dead-house here, clasped hands and were drowned together, the chief sister, a gaunt woman six feet high, calling out loud and often 'O Christ, come quickly!' till the end came. The shrieks and sobbing of women and children are described by the survivors as agonizing."

Writing to Reverend R. W. Dixon, an Anglican priest and poet and former teacher of his at Highgate School, Hopkins noted that: "You ask, do I write verse myself. What I had written I burnt before I became a Jesuit and resolved to write no more, as not belonging to my profession, unless it were by the wish of my superiors; so for seven years I wrote nothing but two or three little presentation pieces which occasion called for. But when in the winter of '75 the Deutschland was wrecked in the mouth of the Thames. . .I was affected by the account and happening to say so to my rector he said that he wished someone would write a poem on the subject. On this hint I set to work and, though my hand was out at first, produced one. I had long had haunting my ear the echo of a new rhythm which now I realised on paper."

We don't know when Hopkins actually completed "The Wreck of the Deutschland." But on the 26th of June, 1876 he was writing his mother that his oldest Jesuit friend, the managing editor of *The Month*, saw no reason not the print the ode in the August issue if it "rhymed and scanned and construed and did not make nonsense or bad morality." However, a subeditor at the journal was asked to judge "The Wreck," and it was that Jesuit's opinion that the thirty-five esoteric stanzas were hardly readable and had only managed to give him a headache. And so the handwritten pages were eventually returned to Hopkins with regrets.

That was as close as Hopkins ever got to seeing his glorious and stunningly original poetry published. Sonnets such as "Pied Beauty," "The Windhover," and "God's Grandeur" have since become regular entries in anthologies of English literature, but they were not collected into a book, plainly titled *Poems*, until 1918, nearly three decades after Hopkins died of typhoid in Dublin at age forty-four.

My historical novel *Exiles* braids together a narrative of the five nuns onboard the *Deutschland* and a narrative of Hopkins's saintly and somewhat thwarted life as he was increasingly afflicted by overwork and what seems to have been psychological depression. Exiled from his Oxford classmates, his family, and Britain itself by his conversion to Catholicism and his Jesuit vows, Hopkins ended up teaching Classics in Ireland, where the English were scorned and where he penned a poem whose first line was "To seem the stranger lies my lot, my life."

I was fascinated by the ways in which a shipwreck that inspired Hopkins's renewed interest in poetry could become a metaphor for his foundering life. But though family and friends considered his years after Oxford wasted, we know that there was a final victory, and that Hopkins's works of genius, through God's grace, were not lost.

# TRUE CRIME

## Writing *A Wild Surge of Guilty Passion*

A FEW YEARS AGO I TAUGHT A SENIOR SEMINAR ON FILM NOIR FOR THE English Department. Our fourth week in the course was devoted to James M. Cain's short novel *Double Indemnity*, and to the fine 1944 Billy Wilder film adaptation starring Fred MacMurray, Barbara Stanwyck, and Edward G. Robinson, with a script by Wilder and Raymond Chandler. In both the novel and movie, a California insurance salesman meets the strange and alluring wife of one of his wealthy clients, finds out she wants to get rid of her husband, and hardly hesitates before deciding to help her do it. Walter knows that the insurance policy pays double its value for accidental loss of life, so he and Phyllis fraudulently get the husband to sign for a hefty amount and plot to make it appear the husband Walter, who in fact was bludgeoned in his car, fell in a deadly way off a train. They garner no suspicions from the police but Walter's superior at work, a crafty investigator for the insurance company, is soon on the case, and all goes downhill from there.

In preparing for class, I read a biography of James M. Cain and found a tiny footnote that indicated the plot was based "on the Snyder/ Gray case." That was all. I had heard nothing whatsoever of the case, but through the magic of Google I found Wikipedia and other entries that gave a general background on the love affair between Judd Gray and Ruth Snyder that resulted in the 1927, Queens, New York homicide of Ruth's husband, Albert Snyder, the art editor of *Motorboating Magazine*.

Screenwriter William Goldman used to say that in pitching a movie to Hollywood studios the screenwriter should say the project would be "just like" some masterpiece "but completely different." The same holds true for those who focus on writing historical fiction: we chance upon a once-well-known topic that has enormous but inviting gaps in its narrative and either has been forgotten or has been reported with gross factual errors. In my historical fiction I have sought to clarify with some particularity how Jesse James was killed by Robert Ford; endeavored to revive Geli Raubal, Hitler's niece, who'd largely disappeared from history but whom he'd claimed was the only woman he ever loved; and I sought to give life to the five nuns featured in British Jesuit poet Gerard Manley Hopkins's "The Wreck of the Deutschland."

The Snyder/Gray case was, for me, equally compelling.

Even now some Internet postings are just plain wrong about multiple aspects of a Snyder/Gray murder case that in the late twenties was called "the crime of the century." I corroborated some information by researching library microfilms of *The New York Times* and *The New York Daily Mirror* for 1927, and I was helped enormously by an edited transcript of the Queens County trial, by Judd Gray's memoir *Doomed Ship*—finished just minutes before his execution in Sing Sing's electric chair—and by Ruth Snyder's crazy, serialized, jailhouse rant, *My Own True Story—So Help Me God!*

My own fascination had less to do with the details of the homicide than with the deadly progress of an eighteen-month love affair between a fun-loving, sultry, irresistible housewife and a suave, small, dandyish corset salesman who would jointly register over fifty times for a clandestine room in the old Waldorf-Astoria—where the Empire State Building is now—and gradually find themselves conspiring to kill Albert, whom Ruth called "the old crab," a cultured, sour, loveless artist whom Judd had never met.

The novel is not a whodunit. Even the book jacket itself gives away those facts typically withheld in mysteries. The interest for me was in the psychology behind Ruth's fantasy of perfect happiness once her husband was done away with and she received the $96,000 in insurance money—an enormous sum then—that she'd deceptively got Albert to give his signature to, and Judd's slavish devotion to his strong-willed lover, letting lust, lots of whisky, and his own pliant nature determine what he would do.

The fun of writing historical fiction is finding out new things all the time. At a Christmas party, I asked Tim Healy of Electrical Engineering what the green tint was on the copper roof of the old Waldorf-Astoria, and the next morning received an e-mail from him telling me it was a patina called verdigris. With this book I also discovered that in 1925 Noxema was called Dr. Bunting's Sunburn Remedy; cars were still without heaters or radios; hip flasks and lipstick first became fashionable; the term "bimbo" referred to a man, not a woman; Mayor Jimmy Walker made it possible to watch movies on Sundays; most people worked six days a week; and even though it was the era of Prohibition, someone arriving at the Port Authority Terminal in New York City could find illegal alcohol for sale in less than a minute.

Also surprising was the speed of the justice system then. Judd and Ruth murdered a sleeping Albert with a five-pound sash weight in the wee hours of Sunday, March 20th. Both were in jail by Monday night. The first interviews with jurors took place on April 18th; the trial—which was as famous then as O. J. Simpson's was in our time—took only seventeen days; Albert Snyder's own character was never called into question; and even with appeals, the lovers were executed in Sing Sing just seven months after their sentencing. (I got a sense of Ruth's skylark nature when I found out that sentencing took place on May 13th and Ruth joked to a jailer, "This is my worst Friday the 13th ever.")

All during the two years or so that I was writing the novel I was waiting for a title and I finally found it in a newspaper editorial written by Cornelius Vanderbilt III just after the couple were arrested. He wrote: "The instinct of motherhood, the desire of a father to shield his child from harm, common sense, any feeling of decency toward a loving mate were all swept away before a wild surge of guilty passion."

Of such Aha! moments are novels made.

# THE MAKING OF AN OUTLAW

## Writing *The Kid*

I FIRST WAS ATTRACTED TO THE IDEA OF A NOVEL ABOUT WILLIAM H. Bonney after reading Stephen Tatum's *Inventing Billy the Kid*, in which he demonstrates that each generation has its own conception of the outlaw. The journalists of his day who'd never met or even seen him from afar depicted him as a vicious, satanic, half-animal, whereas those who did interview him were disarmed by his good looks, jocularity, and overall pleasantness. Memoirs about him by friends like Dr. Henry Hoyt and George Coe also paint a sympathetic portrait of a young, rootless orphan caught up in a Wild West civil war and eking out a life just as many others did—even Sheriff Pat Garrett—by rustling calves and horses from the vast herds roaming freely in the still raw and unfenced New Mexico Territory.

And then there's that photograph of him, looking like a slovenly, somewhat effeminate sad sack in his ill-fitting clothes and semi-crushed hat. All the very rare photographic portraits of the period feature ordinary people in their finest duds, usually with weaponry on display. And it hit me that this reportedly natty dresser purposely went the other way in his pose, choosing to be different, to be unlike the others in queue for the cameraman, his melancholia and frail self-esteem insisting that he be noticed in whatever way was easiest.

I was particularly impressed by the letters the Kid wrote to Governor Lew Wallace in his effort to have Wallace honor his earlier promise and give him clemency for testifying against himself. Billy had only a few years of formal schooling, yet the handwriting, the spelling, and the thoughtfulness in the letters are those of a smart, yearning, and earnest twenty-year-old seeking a way out of crime. Reading everything I could about the Kid, I only found myself liking him more and wishing he'd had a father or mentor—which he persistently sought—in order to show him the right path. The older men he did find and admire were all soon killed.

That the Kid was shot dead by Pat Garrett at age twenty-one just made him a more romantic figure and a kind of misunderstood, all-American swashbuckler of the type boys play in the yard. A half-year before the Kid died, a journalist alluded to the folk tale *Ali Baba and the Forty Thieves* in trying to illustrate the public's rapt perception of him. The Kid was in fact what we'd call a petty thief, but one who is ascertained as having killed, for sure, four men, two of them in self-defense and two when he was escaping jail two weeks before his ordered execution.

Yet Billy the Kid has become an internationally known personality because of the power of myth and our own creative imaginations. We certainly see that when we note that newspapers in Chicago, New York, and London all carried articles about his sudden death, and when we count no less than four dime novels soon playing off his life for the authors' own inventions. It was primarily in response to them that Pat Garrett, with his friend Ash Upson, wrote *The Authentic Life of Billy the Kid, the Noted Desperado* in 1882, only to have it sell far worse that the outright fictions about Billy.

As a journalist says in John Ford's *The Man Who Shot Liberty Valance*, "This is the West, sir. When the fact becomes legend, print the legend. "

IV

# GOODBYE TO ALL THAT

## Thomas Merton's *My Argument with the Gestapo*

IN A SMART, GLORIOUS, REVIEW-TO-DIE-FOR IN *THE NEW YORK TIMES* IN 1969, John Leonard wrote of *My Argument with the Gestapo* that the late Thomas Merton in 1941 used the war in Europe "as a private Rorschach, the self as a reel locked into a projection booth, while bombs come down on the movie-house. For beyond the buffoonery is a horror (abstract, impersonal) he couldn't guess at while he wrote. And beyond language . . . is silence, the silence he sought in his monastic vows, the silence he forsook to write *The Seven Storey Mountain*, the poems, the Vietnam protests."

The two primary things that preoccupied Tom Merton in 1941 were his deep and compelling yearning for religious life and the Roman Catholic priesthood, awakened around the time of his conversion and baptism in 1938, as well as, of course, the world-wide slaughter in what would finally be called World War II. His seemingly escapist response to those issues was to write what he then called *The Journal of My Escape from the Nazis*.

What follows is the biography of that novel showing that its fictional scenes in the London and Paris caught up in war are in fact a psychogenic meditation on the state of the world and of the author's own warring soul, functioning as a factual examination of his past just as it evinced his hopes for silence and seclusion in a Trappist future.

\*\*\*

In 1933 Germany's 85-year-old president, Paul von Hindenburg, had appointed the Austrian Adolf Hitler as his Chancellor in a panicky appeasement of the increasingly violent National Socialist German Workers' party, of which Hitler was the unquestioned leader. Within months the Nazis intimidated, silenced, or assassinated all their competitors and became the only legal political party in the nation. And after Hindenburg's death, with stunning speed Hitler took over the government, withdrew from the League of Nations, seized lands he felt were stolen from Germany by World War I's Treaty of Versailles, and otherwise violated that accord by creating a *Luftwaffe*, or air force, growing the *Wehrmacht* to a final number of 18 million soldiers, sailors, and airmen, signing pacts with Italy and Japan, annexing Austria to Germany, and otherwise readying the nation for a war that sought *Lebensraum*, "living space," in Eastern Europe.

A helpless world watched. In September 1939, Hitler's forces invaded Poland, prompting Great Britain and France to finally declare war. Germany responded with a punishing strategy of *blitzkrieg* against London, and in 1940 France was swiftly conquered and occupied by the *Wehrmacht*, which installed a puppet government at Vichy.

Wearied by the first World War, and just rising up out of the Great Depression, the United States tried to stay out of the conflict, though Congress did pass the Lend Lease Act in March 1941, which provided military aid to the foreign nations dealing with the Axis onslaught.

All of this would have been front page news from Tom's first year at Columbia University in 1934 through the completion of his 1939 Master's thesis on "Nature and Art in William Blake." And the pacifist in him could only have been jarred and resentful over the fact that the homes of his youth in France and England were caught up in declarations of war.

Tom's first acquaintance with the Nazis, at age 17, is recalled in the "Author's Preface" to *My Argument with the Gestapo*. "One Sunday morning in the spring of 1932," he wrote, "I was hiking through the Rhine Valley. With a pack on my back I was wandering down a quiet country road among flowering apple orchards, near Koblenz. Suddenly a car appeared and came down the road very fast. It was jammed with people. Almost before I had taken full notice of it, I realized it was coming straight at me and instinctively jumped into the ditch. The car passed in a cloud of leaflets and from the ditch I glimpsed its occupants, six or seven youths screaming and shaking their fists. They were Nazis, and it was election day. I was being invited to vote for Hitler, who was not yet in power. These were future officers in the SS. They vanished quickly. The road was once again perfectly silent and peaceful. But it was not the same road as before. It was now a road on which seven men had expressed their readiness to destroy me."

That readiness to destroy was now world-wide, and Tom sought to do exactly the opposite. Saint Francis of Assisi prayed, "Lord, make me an instrument of your peace," and that may have nudged Tom into following the counsel of Dan Walsh, a visiting professor of medieval philosophy at Columbia, to consider a vocation to the priesthood in the Order of Friars Minor, the Franciscans. And so in October 1939, his baptism and confirmation as a Catholic not yet a year old, Tom went to see Father Edmund Murphy, the Order's provincial secretary, then in residence at the Church of Saint Francis of Assisi on 31st Street. Murphy was a hail-fellow-well-met who recognized Tom's piety, intelligence, and merry-eyed charm, and heartened him by saying he could foresee Tom joining fellow postulants at the novitiate of Saint Anthony in August 1940.

Elated, Tom designed a daily routine that imitated the Franciscan ordo while continuing his studies for a doctorate in English literature at Columbia, with hopes of a dissertation on the religious poetry of the Jesuit Gerard Manley Hopkins.

In 1939 Tom had begun an autobiographical novel that swelled to five hundred pages and was first titled *The Straits of Dover,* revised and renamed as *The Night Before the Battle,* and finally, after much surgery on the narrative, was called *The Labyrinth*. While teaching classes in English composition at Columbia Extension School, he sought a publisher for the novel, submitting the typescript first to Farrar and Rinehart, then Macmillan, Viking, Alfred A. Knopf, and Harcourt Brace, where junior editor Robert Giroux, an old friend from Columbia who later would become the editor of *The Seven Storey Mountain,* later recalled in print that this version of the mutable book was titled *The Straits of Dover* and concerned a Cambridge Englishman who transferred to Columbia and got "involved with a stupid millionaire, a show girl, a Hindu mystic and a left-winger in Greenwich Village. I agreed with the other editors," Giroux wrote, "that the author had talent but the story wobbled and got nowhere."

Either the rejections or his doctoral studies seem to have stalled Tom for a time and he seems not to have returned to fiction writing even in the summer of 1940 when he again vacationed at the hillside cottage owned by Bob Lax's brother-in-law. Joining Lax and Tom that summer were also Eddie Rice, Jim McKnight, Sy Freedgood, Bob Gibney, and Bob Gerdy. Each had been associated with Columbia's undergraduate journal, *Jester*, and each wanted to be a writer, so they'd hauled their L. C. Smith and Royal portable typewriters up to the cottage to hammer out novels, listen to jazz, drink to excess, party with the pretty New York City girls who visited, and wrangle over just and unjust wars and the world's impending doom.

Still looking forward to becoming a Franciscan friar, Tom was often off by himself meditating in the woods, reciting the rosary, or reading the *Summa Theologica* of Saint Thomas Aquinas. But with the cottage so over-populated, in June Tom walked down to Saint Bonaventure College, then an all-male Franciscan school on five hundred pastoral acres near the city of Olean, and on the presumption of his entrance into the Saint Anthony novitiate in August he was permitted a room in the dormitory and got to know the friars while studying Franciscan history and practicing their way of life.

Yet he was assailed by shame over his past sinfulness, especially at Cambridge University where he'd roistered and sired a child out of wedlock, the very scandal that provoked his English guardian to send him across the Atlantic to Columbia after his freshman year, and Tom was aware he hadn't confessed such wickedness to the provincial secretary. So he took a grim train ride to the city and again interviewed with Father Edmund Murphy, penitently laying out the exact nature of his wrongs. And the worst possible outcome he could imagine was realized when an otherwise friendly, kindly, but shocked Father Murphy told him to withdraw his application to the Franciscans. Weeping and remorseful, Tom went for consolation to the sacrament of penance, confessing his misery to a Capuchin priest who jumped to conclusions about the religious hysteric beyond the grill and in irritation said his pursuit of Holy Orders was henceforth out of the question.

His yearned-for vocation to the cloister and ordination seemingly in ruins, Tom still professed his undying loyalty to the Friars Minor and returned to Olean. And in a second-best solution, he was hired to teach three fall classes of a sophomore English literature survey at Saint Bonaventure College where, he wrote, "the salary I got was quite sufficient to enable me to practice evangelical poverty" and where he would reside in Devereaux Hall with, as he called them, "football players with long, unpronounceable names."

In the fall of 1940, Tom wrote a novel entitled *The Man in the Sycamore Tree* about a character very like himself who, as Paul M. Pearson describes him, "writes stories and poems, is working on an MA on Blake, reads Gilson and Maritain, is melancholy, very pious, greatly troubled by the news from Europe, and is attracted to the priestly life." The book was rejected by his literary agency Curtis, Brown and he himself admitted it was not very good. But he wrote, "So many bad books get printed, why can't *my* bad book get printed?"

And in November he viewed a nine-minute British propaganda film, *London Can Take It!*, that depicted eighteen hours of *Luftwaffe* bombers— London's "nightly visitors"—systematically devastating five centuries of civilization in an effort to undermine Britain's morale. The documentary stated that the blitzes fostered the opposite effect as the stiff-upper-lip citizens kept to their ordinary chores and routines each morning, ever more determined to resist.

The first seeds of *The Journal of My Escape from the Nazis* may have been planted then. "Bombs are beginning to fall into my life," Tom wrote in a journal entry. "That wasn't true with Warsaw. I had never seen, nor imagined, Warsaw. But more terrible was seeing the line of people going down into the air raid shelter at dusk. Then seeing the empty streets, and an air raid warden walking slowly with his hands behind him, in the sudden flash of a bomb: and hearing the sound of that air raid alarm. This, for the first time, made me want to fight."

Soon after his 26th birthday, Tom became a lay member of the Franciscan Third Order, with the intent of living like a monk in the world, continuing his regimen of Masses and confession, but also renouncing politics, giving up cigarettes, alcohol, and meat, wearing a brown scapular, and reciting the seven canonical hours, or Office, from his Latin breviaries. And at some crucial point he again met with his mentor Dan Walsh and heard the professor describe with zeal the stirring retreats he took at the Cistercian Abbey of Our Lady of Gethsemani. His enthusiasm was enough to excite Tom into registering to go to Kentucky in April to be with the Trappists for Holy Week.

"As soon as I thought about it," he wrote in his journal, "I saw that this was the only choice. That was where I needed to go. Something had opened out, inside me, in the last months, something that required, demanded at least a week in that silence, in that austerity, praying together with the monks in their cold choir. And my heart expanded with anticipation and happiness."

As could have been expected, Tom was overwhelmed by the Holy Week experience, maintaining he'd been residing there in "the palace of the Queen of Heaven." In *The Seven Mountains of Thomas Merton*, biographer Michael Mott points out that in the seven days that Tom was at Gethsemani "he wrote twenty-three pages in the large journal in celebration of the greatest discovery of his life. In terms of a sort of sustained rapture nothing would ever be quite like this again."

Revealing then, that three weeks later, on May 6th, Tom began his last sustained work of fiction, *The Journal of My Escape from the Nazis*. In *The Seven Storey Mountain* Tom wrote that the *Journal* was "the kind of book that I liked to write, full of double-talk and all kinds of fancy ideas that sounded like Franz Kafka. One reason why it was satisfying was that it fulfilled a kind of psychological necessity that had been pent up in me all through the last stages of the war because of my identification, by guilt, with what was going on in England.

"So I put myself there and, telescoping my own past with the air-raids that were actually taking place as its result, I wrote this journal. And, as I say, it was something that I needed to write."

Even though he was teaching a summer school session on Bibliography, mostly to nuns, he must have maintained a high-speed output of some twelve to fifteen pages per day, for as soon as June 11th he wrote in his journal that a first draft of the novel was "already in the hands of Miss Burton," his agent at Curtis, Brown. She may have gently commented on it in a way that urged him to revise, and on July 6th, like a guileless undergraduate in his first fiction writing class, he noted that his novel-in-progress "has a definite form: things seem to have to start in a certain way and what I write has to have some conscious reference to something

I wrote the day before: there is enough of a thread of connection to be embarrassing." He added, "It will never sell, because of the Esperanto," and he was sorry that he hadn't taken more care with the novel, "instead of just writing it carelessly from day to day, like any journal, which is what I wanted at first. Since it can't be sold, why not write completely at your ease? Simply because I can't write for fun."

Tom considered the novel finally finished on the feast of St. Clare, August 12th, and sent part of it to Chester Kerr, an editor at *The Atlantic Monthly Press*, who professed that he liked it but thought it wasn't commercial. "What's commercial?" Tom journaled. "Even if the word means something to him, even then he isn't right. Publishers must be crazy. On the other hand, what does publication matter anyway?"

That final question had much to do with his flirtations with either helping the Russian baroness who'd founded Friendship House in Harlem or forging ahead with the effort to join the Order of Cistercians of the Strict Observance. The choice became simplified when, on the Friday after Thanksgiving, he had a luncheon meeting at the Columbia Faculty Club with Mark Van Doren. Their talk generally focused on Van Doren's reading of *The Journal of My Escape from the Nazis*, but on exiting the club the English professor, who was not a Catholic, off-handedly asked whatever became of Tom's hope of becoming a priest.

Tom could only shrug.

Van Doren told him that the fact that he had let the idea of ordination fall away following just one rebuff may have meant he had no vocation after all.

Silently, Tom rejected that notion, for his longing felt permanent, but he recognized he may have been delaying and dilly-dallying and it was high time to strive in earnest for his deepest desire. Taking leave of the professor on 116th Street, he told him, "If I ever entered any monastery, it would be to become a Trappist."

In fact, *which* religious community he'd join was now not the aching question for him; it was about the possibility of Holy Orders itself. But then one night he found his philosopher friend, Father Philotheus, and shared his dire questions. Tom wrote of that meeting, "Instantly he says that, in his opinion, there is no canonical impediment in my case." And he advised that Tom go again to Gethsemani as soon as the semester's

Christmas vacation began and confess his problematic past and current inclination to the Abbot, Dom Frederic Dunne.

Still hedging a little, Tom wrote to request only a Christmas retreat with the Trappists, though he hinted that entrance as a postulant would be a consideration.

And then on December 7th the Imperial Japanese bombed the Pearl Harbor naval base, and on the feast of the Immaculate Conception Adolf Hitler joined Japan in declaring war against the United States. And though it would seem like he was fleeing in cowardly fashion what he called "the universal penance of military service and the war," Tom needed out of an ever more chaotic and noisome world that too often seemed to want nothing at all to do with holiness and God.

There followed a hurricane of activity as Tom arranged for other faculty to take over his English classes, shipped a closetful of clothes to Friendship House, gave away books and papers to the Saint Bonaventure Library, sent his poems, journals, and *The Journal of My Escape from the Nazis* to Mark Van Doren for safe keeping, watched flames consume his other novel manuscripts, and filled just one suitcase with what Army recruits call "civies" and which he hoped to soon replace with clerical attire.

When Naomi Burton heard from Robert Lax that Tom was joining the Trappists, the agent said in loss and misery, "Oh God. He'll never write again."

***

She was quite wrong. Tom entered the Abbey on December 10th, was received into the novitiate on February 21st, 1942, and in 1944 his *Thirty Poems* was published. Three books by him came out in 1946 just as *The Seven Storey Mountain* was accepted by Bob Giroux at Harcourt Brace. And that autobiography became, of course, a phenomenon, selling six hundred thousand copies in its first year and earning its silent, cloistered, contemplative monk an unpredictable international fame as he readied for Holy Orders on May 25th. And from then on, though he was given some minor chores like orientation classes for novices or the newly invented role of Master of Scholastics, his main job, and a tremendous source of income for the Abbey, was his prolific writing: he averaged at least one book a year and published as many as six titles in 1948, five in 1949, four in 1953, four in 1956, five in 1958, and so on.

Even though he still thought it a great loss that *The Journal of My Escape from the Nazis* was not in print, he seemed to have forgotten about trying to get the novel published until the Vietnam War was at its hottest and the peace-seeking Trappist sought a way to reorient the public mind. The first journal mention of his new hopes for the book appeared in 1967, on September 9th, when he recorded that: "I wanted to collect my thoughts but had to work in the afternoon finishing a re-reading of the *Journal of My Escape from the Nazis*, which I want to get copied and submit for publication after all these years."

Writing about the novel in his journal entry for February 8th, 1968, he noted that the typed manuscript of *The Journal of My Escape from the Nazis* seemed to have fallen to the floor and been put back together incorrectly so that incidents were confusingly out of order. But he wrote: "Whatever the mess—this is a book I am pleased with—this *Journal of Escape*. I have always thought of it as one of my best. Not that it holds together perfectly as a book, but there is good writing and it comes from the center where I have really experienced myself and my life. It represents a very vital and crucial—and fruitful—moment of my existence. Perhaps now I am turning to some such moment of breakthrough. I hope I am. I won't have many more chances!"

In 1968, an ominous last sentence.

On May 14th he wrote: "There was a letter from Naomi Burton who said that the *Journal of the Escape from the Nazis* passes from hand to hand at Doubleday and nobody knows what to make of it. She likes it but the rest are idiots."

On June 23rd he wrote: "Though there is very little enthusiasm at Doubleday over *Journal of My Escape*, Naomi has been authorized to make me an offer and I am accepting it. Maybe I'm wrong. I think Doubleday is a bunch of nitwits. But Naomi likes the book and has fought hard for it—will continue to."

Just a day later, Tom could write, "I have accepted an offer from Doubleday for *Journal of My Escape from the Nazis*, though they are very cool towards it for the most part. Yet Naomi is for it and so is one other senior editor."

Without prompting, in a letter to his agent on June 26th, he recorded a major change: "The reshuffled [manuscript] is on the way to the NY office with a new title: *My Argument with the Gestapo.* Could be subtitled 'A Macaronic Journal' 1941."

"Macaronic" or his other term "Esperanto" refers to the occasional mixture of Romance languages, German, and street English in a zany concoction borne of the tomfoolery of James Joyce and P. G. Wodehouse. I found the passages unrewarding to puzzle out and easy to skip past. A more confident editor would have excised them.

In one of Tom's last journal entries, written in India on the 24th of November, he noted the title change but offered no further explanation for it, saying only: "Naomi Burton is going ahead with the publication of *My Argument with the Gestapo* at Doubleday. She wants a preface by W. H. Auden or Robert Lowell, the poets."

That *The Journal of My Escape from the Nazis* seems to have been impulsively retitled *My Argument with the Gestapo* possibly indicates that he first of all sought to differentiate the novel from the serially published journals that he suspected were the height of his literary achievement, and he may have wanted the hints of suspicion and danger associated with the Gestapo. But it must be said that neither title is wholly accurate or telling about the contents of his book. The first implies an imprisonment by the SS and perhaps a feat of derring-do worthy of Steve McQueen on his fence-leaping motorcycle in *The Great Escape.* And *My Argument with the Gestapo* conjures up humorless secret police circled around a shackled man sitting under a glare of light as he disputes with a merciless interrogator. There would have been a wider audience for such pulp fiction; it could have resembled the John Buchan spy thrillers that Tom avidly read as a teen in England. But Tom had to rely on his later worldwide celebrity rather than his characterizations or plotting to sell this particular book. As Monica Furlong noted in *Merton: A Biography,* his *My Argument with the Gestapo* was "a fascinating book, often brilliantly written in a rather Joycean style, and deeply interesting to those interested in Merton. It does not really work as a novel, being unsteadily poised between fiction and autobiography, having neither the unity of the first nor the simple factual basis of the second."

***

The narrator of *My Argument with the Gestapo* is Thomas James Merton, born like Tom in Prades, France on January 31st, 1915. Tom's finest entries in the narrative are deeply felt recollections of his childhood in France and his seven years in England, but the book is otherwise an imaginary journey to those countries by a vigilant, perplexed, not quite American spectator who's often mistaken for a spy. He tells an officer interrogating him about biographical details, "If you want to identify me, ask me not where I live, or what I like to eat, or how I comb my hair, but ask me what I think I am living for, in detail, and ask me what I think is keeping me from living fully for the thing I want to live for."

The secular world was not asking those questions, but his heart was.

In the "Author's Preface," Tom wrote, "This novel is a kind of sardonic meditation on the world in which I then found myself: an attempt to define its predicament and my own place in it." A paragraph later he added, "The reader must remember that it was dreamed in 1941, and that its tone of divertissement marks it as a document of a past era," by which he means there is no awareness of the concentration camps or Nazi massacres.

The initial difficulty in getting the manuscript published in 1941 was exactly "that it was dreamed" when during that same period a host of reporters and filmmakers were vividly recording the stunning, harsh, life-altering realities of World War II in London and the Occupation. But few of those journalists could match the lilting cadence and concrete imagery of Tom's poetic prose. When asked by an ex-girlfriend what he will say of London, the character Thomas Merton states, "I will write about the small room I once slept in, one that smelled of fog and quilts, in a temperance place. All night long I could hear water murmuring in the pipes in the wall, and the voices of old ladies came through the frail locked door—thin voices of people roaming quietly on the stairs like wraiths in *The Aeneid*, gathering around a saucer of blood."

With an epigraph by John Donne, and allusions to Dante Alighieri, William Blake, T. S. Eliot, James Joyce, and Evelyn Waugh, it's the kind of book that many a doctoral student in English literature could have hoped to write. But Tom was far more than them a gifted natural as a narrator, as when he descriptively lists the high points and low of his matriculation at

Clare College, Cambridge: "I visited the proctor, in his rooms in the new court at Magdalen, and paid him a fine for not having a square. I had tea with some girls at Girton, sitting under a tree in some fairly long grass, in the untidy part of the grounds. I had a friend who grew a beard. I read some of the works of the divine Dante. I was gated for ten days in the Lent term, for being drunk. I did cartoons in the *Granta* and the *Gownsman*. I sat in the writing room of the Union and wrote short, boastful letters to my younger brother, and from the library of the Union I borrowed Cocteau's *Thomas l'Imposteur*, Stendahl's *De l'Amour*, and Flaubert's *L'Education sentimentale*."

Thomas Merton, the character, is in London in 1941 "to see what is happening" and he's rooming in the house of the cultured, wealthy, worldly-wise Madame Gongora and her Spanish bodyguard when he happens to meet, too briefly, B., his old girlfriend, and here a sly nod to Dante's Beatrice. Much changed now and forced into helmet and uniform, B. inspires reminiscences of the Oakham school in Rutland, dear friends he'd had, Charlie Chaplin films, and Anglican church services he'd grudgingly attended, preferring in contrast the candled and incensed mysteries of the Catholic Mass and the discipline and integrity of the Trappists. The author's only allusion to what caused the Franciscans to reject his candidacy is off-handedly offered in a confession to a British agent in which he tells him "that I several times went out with a girl who was known all over Cambridge as the 'Freshman's delight.'"

Tom called the novel "a kind of sardonic meditation on the world in which I then found myself," and that scornful derision in 1941 made the abnegations and erasures of monastic life far more welcome. Tom's own critique of the novel in 1951 was that, "One of the problems of the book was my personal relation to the world and to the war. When I wrote it, I thought I had a very supernatural solution. After nine years in the monastery I see that this was no solution at all. The false solution was this: the whole world, of which the war is a characteristic expression, is evil. It has, therefore, to be first ridiculed, then spat upon, and at last formally cursed."

There is a good riddance and goodbye-to-all-that quality to his memories of London, as if the rubble and destruction have laid bare what was licentious, stupid, tawdry, cruel, and hidden with shame behind a falsely respectable façade. And the journalist either imagines or is in fact being tailed by lurking detectives or investigators of unknown origin who suspect he's up to no good. The predicament that Tom was in was that of ridiculing or formally cursing the secular world as he felt an ever-greater affinity for a buried life that seemed to contradict and deny all his writerly ambitions.

Worried about deportation or prison, in the novel Thomas Merton crosses the English Channel in a torpedo boat, transfers onto a French fishing boat near Deauville, and hitches a ride to Abbeville in a truck full of happy German soldiers who claim their life is a dream, who feel forever young. Those jolly scamps are the only Nazis he ever encounters in the book.

In Paris the narrator hides out in the Hotel Rocamadour, where Tom and his father, Owen, stayed in more palmy days. Again, he's questioned by detectives, "big, thick-necked brutal men, Frenchmen that look and behave exactly like Germans."

Editor Bob Giroux recalled that in the first novel he'd read by Tom "the story wobbled and got nowhere." And so it is with *My Argument with the Gestapo*. Our protagonist has his journal stolen and perused by censors and then is "led off to the investigation from which, to my great surprise, I emerged more or less free to go about in Paris as I pleased." It would thus seem a shaggy dog story in which a rambling narrative leads to an inconsequential ending in which the Gestapo is never really run afoul of.

The English novelist E. M. Forster famously taught that, "The king died and then the queen died is a story. The king died, and then the queen died of grief is a plot." We have no real plot in *My Argument with the Gestapo*, just a sequence of happenings, like glimpses of outdoor life from a hurtling passenger train. And the novel concludes not with an escape from the Nazis or an argument with the Gestapo, but a Kafkaesque conversation with an American correspondent for newspapers and broadcasting companies who presumes the character's journal is a pornographic diary. Thomas Merton surrenders the manuscript to this "R." in order to have it safely mailed to his New York agent from Lisbon. Meanwhile, he chooses to remain in France, his first home, and the home too, of course, of the first Cistercian monastery, La Grande Trappe. Even if unconscious, such connections could not have been out of Tom's mind. And he thinks of the poet William Blake "filling paper with words, so that the words flew about the room for the angels to read, and after that, what if the paper was lost or destroyed?

"That is the only reason for wanting to write, Blake's reason."

In *The New York Times* of July 10, 1969, John Leonard extolled *My Argument with the Gestapo* by noting: "Compounded in equal parts of autobiography, spiritual passage and incantatory tour de force, it is less a conventional novel than the word drunk, panic stricken, sorrowful-hilarious journal of a man hounded by and hounding after the idea of God."

That "hounded by and hounding after" is a crucial insight about an intriguing and exuberant novel-like thing originally composed during a period of intense spiritual torment. "It was something that I needed to write," Tom said. A sort of exorcism. Seen in that way, the Gestapo represent all the negative, policing, scoffing enemies of religious life who sought to impede and undermine his vocation, letting him shirk the responsibilities of his calling.

*My Argument* can be viewed as an interior monologue about Tom's conflicted hankering, vacillation, uncertainty, and the naysaying voices that seemed to be railing against him. And *The Journal of My Escape from the Nazis* was essentially a journal of his wistful intention to find solitude, renounce the world, and give up everything, even his writing talent, for a God who was the *Solus Tuus*, or "Only You," that then really mattered to him.

# A LOST PRIESTHOOD

## Edwin O'Connor's *The Edge of Sadness*

WE OWNED A SHELF OF READER'S DIGEST CONDENSED BOOKS WHEN I was in high school, but the family hardbacks were limited to a handsomely illustrated and mostly unread Bible, and *Too Late the Phalarope* by Alan Paton, *Not as a Stranger* by Morton Thompson, and *The Edge of Sadness* by Edwin O'Connor.

Each of those novels was a critically-acclaimed bestseller in its time—*The Edge of Sadness* won the 1962 Pulitzer Prize for fiction—but only *The Edge of Sadness* had fallen out of print until its welcome resuscitation as a Loyola Classic.

Some books are so much of their age that they can quickly seem as quaint, old-fashioned, and neuralgic as foxtrot tunes. And that, I think, was the fate of *The Edge of Sadness* after Vatican Council II (1962—1965). Widely regarded as the most significant religious event in the Roman Catholic Church since the sixteenth-century Reformation, the post-Council Church sought to reconstruct a Catholicism personified in O'Connor's novel by the Saint Raymond's pastor referred to only by his title, Monsignor: "an eccentric, despotic, devout old man who, like so many of the old-time pastors, seemed to have won from his people something which was not love, exactly, but a peculiar kind of exasperated idolatry."

His kind would fade away after Vatican II, as would the Latin Mass that O'Connor's Father Hugh Kennedy "said," facing the tabernacle and generally without the vigilant participation of his congregation. It could be a grand and regal spectacle but it had little to do with the Lord's Supper or the practices of the early Church, and so it was replaced by liturgies in the vernacular in which the aloof and anonymous parishioners of Old Saint Paul's would have been expected to offer in English the responses that grade school altar boys like me had recited in memorized and mispronounced Latin.

And there were other far-reaching changes. The Church was no longer considered just the hierarchy or the clergy, but also the laity, the People of God, who were given a greater role in the management of their parishes. Ecumenism was encouraged. Hymnals were modernized for good and for ill, with some folk Masses becoming indistinguishable from a hootenanny. The harsher codes of canon law were rewritten in a more pastoral way. Religious orders were required to reexamine and, in some cases, alter their rules, their habits, and their ways of proceeding.

The consequence of that happy upheaval was that *The Edge of Sadness* seemed, to many, yesterday's news.

Published five years after the enormous success of his Boston-Irish novel *The Last Hurrah*, Edwin O'Connor's third novel was born out of his close friendships with priests and his deep affection for and fidelity to Catholicism. And his alert, sympathetic, adjudicating intimacy made his book a harbinger of the many things that were wrong in the Church and needed *aggiornamento*—in the Italian term of Pope John XXIII—the act of revision and updating. Because for all its wry asides and vaudevillian comedy, Edwin O'Connor's novel is a profoundly melancholy book about loneliness, lost ideals, and the lack of integrity, whether among vain, crafty, tyrannical capitalists like Charlie Carmody, from whom we expect it, or among affectless, cynical, scandalous priests, from whom we don't.

Even its first paragraph begins with Father Hugh Kennedy's self-denying delusion: "This story at no point becomes my own. I am in it—good heavens, I'm in it to the point of almost never being out of it!—but the story belongs, all of it, to the Carmodys, and my own part, while substantial enough, was never really of any great significance at all."

The book covers a half a year, more or less, in an unnamed city that combines various aspects of Boston, Massachusetts and Providence and Woonsocket, Rhode Island; and its architecture is founded on a rather limited number of scenes that are far longer than in most four-hundred-page novels: a populated birthday party at the Carmody home; conversations with Father John Carmody, Hugh's seminary friend; scenes from the Old Saint Paul's rectory and parish including hilarious dinner table conversations with the zealous, stiff, naïve curate, Father Danowski, and, whenever Hugh can find him, Roy, the lazy, prevaricating janitor; Hugh's memories of his father; a flashback to Hugh's four years recovering from alcoholism at the Cenacle in Arizona; a nostalgic afternoon idyll with Mrs. Helen Carmody O'Donnell, John's kid sister and the one woman from his youth whom Hugh could have imagined marrying; a confessional visit with a seemingly dying Charlie Carmody and, linked to it, a final Saint Raymond's rectory visit with the icy, chastising Father John; and then the inspiring, transporting final pages that signal the surprising, even miraculous, metamorphosis in Hugh.

Edwin O'Connor was born in Providence, Rhode Island on July 29th, 1918, and was raised in affluence in Woonsocket as the oldest son of a highly regarded doctor specializing in internal medicine. His high school was the Christian Brothers' La Salle Academy in Providence—he got there by train each day—and then, in 1935, he went west to South Bend, Indiana and the rigid discipline of the all-male, seeming seminary of the University of Notre Dame du Lac.

A powerful and persistent influence on Edwin O'Connor there was his principal English Department professor, the Frank O'Malley to whom *The Edge of Sadness* is dedicated. O'Connor called him "the greatest single help for me in college," for O'Malley was the charismatic mentor who got the Rhode Island talent to change his major from journalism to English and introduced him to the greatest of the European Catholic philosophers and writers. But O'Connor had observed O'Malley's otherwise wide-ranging and incisive intellect too often fuddled with alcohol, and so he gave Father Hugh Kennedy a similar affliction—O'Connor himself was a teetotaler—in order to provide his friend an example of hope and a way out.

Also crucial to Edwin O'Connor's development as a fiction writer was his fondness for an uncle whose theatrical background extended from vaudeville to the movies, and his own job as a radio announcer between his graduation from Notre Dame in 1939 and his joining the Coast Guard during World War II. A gregarious joker, raconteur, and mimic, O'Connor was enormously attentive to accents and voice, and the speeches and spirited dialogues in his novel need to be read aloud to fully appreciate how good his ear and timing were. And his irony is a joy. Writing about Hugh Kennedy's nighttime walks around a parish that includes Skid Row, O'Connor has the pastor recall a movie scene from the thirties or forties:

It was a scene in which a priest was walking alone at night, through a district which I'm sure was intended to be very much like this one. It was sordid enough, suitably down at the heels, yet in the film it had an odd liveliness: one had the impression of neon and noise and motion. There was a peculiar wailing music in the background, and from the darkness came an occasional scream of violence. Through the shadows one could see the tottering and seedy drunks, the faded streetwalker, the few sharp-eyed hoodlums. And then the priest appeared: an erect man with a steady stride. He was quite handsome. He was also obviously a familiar and impressive neighborhood figure. Although his coat collar was turned up he was recognized at once; the recognition produced a chain reaction of edifying behavior. The drunks managed to straighten themselves and tug respectfully at their hats; the streetwalker, suddenly ashamed, turned away, pointedly fingering the medal at her throat; the hoodlums vanished in their evil Cadillac; the cop on the beat relaxed for the first time, twirled his night stick happily, and hummed a few bars of "The Minstrel Boy." The "padre" was passing by, and the district was the more wholesome for his presence. As for the "padre" himself, he continued to walk forward as strongly as ever, something about him managing to suggest, however, that he was in a dream—a muscular dream. His smile was compassionate but powerful: one had the feeling that here was a mystic from some ecclesiastical gymnasium, a combination of Tarzan and Saint John of the Cross. A saint, but *all man*. . . .

After the war, there was more radio work and free-lance journalism for O'Connor, and he lived hand-to-mouth in Boston even after the publication of his first novel, *The Oracle*. But *The Last Hurrah*, in 1956, made him famous and rich enough that at age thirty-eight he could buy his first car, a Porsche.

Still a suave and affable Irish bachelor, O'Connor became a favorite guest at fashionable dinner parties where he seems to have fallen into the good priest's role of genial interlocutor and generous consort to the otherwise ignored. He became a man of regular habits and haunts, finishing his morning at the typewriter with a stroll to the offices of *The Atlantic Monthly* or his publisher Little, Brown, to be joined by friendly editors in the café of the Ritz Hotel. O'Connor's routine was the sort of thing that fledgling writers dream about and movies too frequently depict but very few actual writers have the book sales or temerity to do it.

Some of his jaunty life is reflected in Father Hugh Kennedy, who may seem to contemporary readers an incredibly carefree, negligent, and un-harried pastor. There is little or no mention in *The Edge of Sadness* of parish councils, club and committee meetings, finance and administration, counseling, choir direction, office help, confessions, baptisms, weddings, and funerals, or contractors called in for repairs. We do not see him reading his breviary. We do not hear him preach—though he implies he does it poorly. Whenever Hugh Kennedy is called on, he seems to be available. That he prays is frequently asserted, but his spirituality is never deeply explored. We learn that he reads John Henry Newman at night; we do not learn which particular books or what nourishment he draws from them.

I have Jesuit friends who report that *The Edge of Sadness* was the first novel they were allowed to read in their novitiate, but it could not have been because it was excellent preparation for the functions and expectations of priesthood. Rather, it must have been selected because it so well describes a very American variation on Saint John of the Cross's *Dark Night of the Soul*.

The greatness of *The Edge of Sadness* lies not in its insider's view of ecclesiastical life, or its portrayal of steely faith, bloody martyrdom, or the heroic struggle to seek out a seemingly ever-withdrawing God. Instead, it lies in its evocation of the age-old maladies of selfishness, lethargy, indifference, and bleakness of soul. One critic, in 1961, called Father Hugh Kennedy "the first dimensionally human priest to emerge from the pages of an American novel." And it is that intensely honest and unsentimental perspective that gives resonance to Edwin O'Connor's novel even today.

# CLOISTERED

## Frank Monaco's *Brothers and Sisters*

CLOSE TO THE MIDDLE OF PHOTOGRAPHER FRANK MONACO'S GLORI-
ous *Brothers and Sisters* there is a picture of a professed sister pinning the
snow-white veil of a novice on a smiling college-age woman who seems
to have just shorn off all her hair. The soft light, the parade behind them
of gray gothic archways, and the harmony and simplicity of the composition suggest an undiscovered painting by the Dutch master Jan Vermeer.
Underneath it is a quotation from St. Teresa of Ávila's sixteenth-century
Carmelite handbook, *Way of Perfection*, that is essential to our understanding of monasticism's attractiveness: "Oh, Sisters, for the love of God,
try to realize what a great favour the Lord has bestowed on us whom he
has brought here."

Love and favor. The happiness that men and women find in con-
secrated, cloistered life is what surprises outsiders most. When, on his
journey to Asia, the Cistercian priest and writer Thomas Merton had a
private meeting with the Dalai Lama, a frustrated man listening at the
door reported that all he could hear was continuous laughter. And on my
occasional visits to monasteries, the lasting impression I have is of happening upon monks in unexpected moments of mirth.

Ascetic religious life in the 21st century would seem to be so lacking
in pleasure and allure that only fools and masochists would choose it. And
indeed the talent and temperament for such a way to holiness seems to
be quite rare. But in the silence of enclosure, the rhythm and orderliness
of routine, the elimination of the distractions and inordinate attachments

of wealth, the abiding constraints of obedience and boundaries, and the selfless and otherworldly focus of the life the soul is at liberty, the spirit is given wings.

Enclosed religious communities fulfill Christ's command to pray without ceasing through the Liturgy of the Hours, a choir recital of hymns, psalms, and biblical or hagiographical readings, that supplies the architecture of their daily existence. Even today, the life of conventual monks and nuns is regulated by a schedule of activities that is fairly similar to that of the Cistercians as Thomas Merton portrayed it fifty years ago in *The Waters of Siloe*:

A.M.

2:00    Rise, go to choir, recite Matins and Lauds of Our Lady's Office.

2:30    Meditation.

3:00    Night Office, which features the canonical hours of Matins and Lauds.

4:00    Priests say their private Masses, others go to Communion. Then there is time for reading or private prayer.

5:30    The hour of Prime, followed by Chapter, which is a community meeting, and possibly a light breakfast (or *frustulum*) of coffee, bread, and occasionally a hard-boiled egg.

6:30    Reading, study, or private prayer.

7:45    The hour of Tierce, High Mass, and the hour of Sext.

9:00    Work or study.

10:45    Reading or prayer.

11:07    None, the fifth of the seven canonical hours.

11:30    The primary meal, consisting of soup, fresh fruit, a side dish of cooked vegetables, bread, and coffee.

P.M.

12:15    Reading or private prayer.

1:30    Work.

3:30    Reading or private prayer.

4:30    The hour of Vespers.

5:15    Meditation.

5:30    Collation, which is some bread, a little fruit, and a hot drink.

5:40    Reading, prayer.

6:10    The hour of Compline, the hymn *Salve Regina*, and examination of conscience.

7:00    All go to bed.

*Ora et labora*, pray and work, was the essence of the Rule of St. Benedict, the sixth century code that provides the fundamental structure for all the religious congregations featured in *Brothers and Sisters*. But a good many photographs in this book also illustrate just how central to monastic culture is reading and the life of the mind; for the sanctuary of cloister is the perfection of a spiritual and intellectual environment for seeking, discerning, intimating, adoring, and resting in the presence of Mystery.

The sisters and brothers in the photographs by Frank Monaco are signs of contradiction. They have found love in celibacy, freedom in discipline, quest in stability, hungers satisfied in a regimen of fasting, needs met in poverty, fulfillment in selflessness, and conversation with holiness in elected silence.

# SHAKESPEARE & ME

IN HIS BOOK *THE WESTERN* CANON, YALE LITERARY CRITIC HAROLD Bloom postulates that William Shakespeare's literary output essentially *is* the canon: that in his time Shakespeare found levels of achievement by which we evaluate all literature now. He is, Bloom has stated, without a precursor and he has since had no equals even though most writers aspire to *be* him. And more: Shakespeare defines for us what we are ourselves and gives us all that we understand of human nature. Human consciousness seems to have been jolted forward about the time of Shakespeare, and he more than others seems to have been aware of what was new. As Harold Bloom points out, Shakespeare is universally adored, in all languages, and perhaps it is for that reason.

In *The New York Times* some years ago there was a story about a huge gathering of Shakespeare scholars and fanciers in a conference hall at which fiction writer Jorge Luis Borges of Argentina was giving the main address. Because Borges was blind, he was escorted onto the stage and to a podium and microphone. But he strayed a little far from that microphone as he began to speak, so that attendees in the front row could hear him, but a thousand others could not. Even craning forward and listening hard, all they could make out was the periodic "Shakespeare," "Shakespeare," "Shakespeare." And yet when Borges finished his talk, the crowd gave him a standing ovation.

In my freshman year in high school I was forced to participate in a talent show. Unwilling to sing or dance and with no gift with musical instruments, I chose to recite Portia's address to Shylock in Act 4 of *The Merchant of Venice,* the lines that read: "The quality of mercy is not

147

strained; it droppeth as the gentle rain of heaven upon the place beneath. It is twice blest . . ." And so on. I suspect I fluttered my fingers overhead to indicate falling rain and suspect I used twinned raised fingers to underscore "twice." A host of gestures all through a long passage I'd memorized. Yes, I was that much a ham.

We had one Shakespeare play assigned during each year of high school: *The Merchant of Venice, Hamlet, Julius Caesar*—handy, since I was learning Latin from his *Gallic Wars*—and *Macbeth*. We also viewed several of Laurence Olivier's wonderful performances of Shakespeare on film.

In college my first course as an English major was on Shakespeare; not all thirty-seven plays but perhaps half that number, and all the 154 sonnets. We read no biographies, no criticism or theory. We just paged through the text as Miss Anderson, with a voice as soft as a cloth wiping a mirror, read aloud something like the stirring speech before battle in *Henry the Fifth:*

> We few, we happy few, we band of brothers;
> For he to-day that sheds his blood with me
> Shall be my brother; be he ne'er so vile
> This day shall gentle his condition:
> And gentlemen in England, now a-bed
> Shall think themselves accursed they were not here,
> And hold their manhoods cheap whiles any speaks
> That fought with us upon Saint Crispin's day.

She'd pause in reflection and gently smile as she asked rhetorically, "Oh, isn't that a beautiful passage?" And then she'd go on.

When I was a Lieutenant in the Army and twenty-two and considered myself immortal, I went to a fly-by-night outfit in Indiana to learn to parachute. The first thing the owners did after accepting my money, which may have been twenty dollars, was have me sign a paper indemnifying them if any loss or injury occurred. The soldier who was with me was a lawyer and he properly balked at signing such a carte blanche agreement, but I was his peer and pressured him, so he cooperated.

To become what the Army calls Airborne requires a three-week course of rigorous exercise and continuous instruction. Yet this civilian operation offered about fifteen minutes on how a parachute works, with another fifteen minutes on jumping from a ladder and hitting the ground in a rolling way that didn't put all the force of a hard fall on just your feet, ankles, and knees.

And then parachutes were strapped onto us. I don't recall even being given a helmet. We got into the back seat of a fixed wing, single-engine, very old airplane, what they call a tail-dragger, and it wouldn't start until the pilot beat on some engine part with a wrench. But then the prop did reach full speed and we coasted onto the tarmac and took off. It was my first ride in such a small plane and in such perilous circumstances and I was both thrilled and wary. And suddenly I found myself remembering the lines from *Julius Caesar*:

> Cowards die many times before their deaths;
> The valiant never taste of death but once.
> Of all the wonders that I yet have heard,
> It seems to me most strange that men should fear;
> Seeing that death, a necessary end,
> Will come when it will come.

I find that remembrance the kind of care-free, stoic, cast-your-fate-into-the-wind attitude that's only possible when young. And Shakespeare the playwright also remembered being that way.

When it was my turn to jump, I left the plane to hold onto a wing brace as I balanced on a small step. My so-called instructor reached out to adjust my stance for some reason, and I took that as a prompt to leap. So I did, immediately pulling my ripcord and feeling the upward tug as the parachute blossomed overhead. I happened to be far away from the drop zone and heading toward a crash onto an Indiana interstate, but at the time I was only hearing the quiet rush of wind in my 24 feet per second descent and marveling at the beauty of Indiana farmland in the fall. And for some reason then I recalled the generous paean to England in Shakespeare's *Richard II*:

> This royal throne of kings, this sceptered isle,
> This earth of majesty, this seat of Mars,
> This other Eden, demi-paradise . . .
> This blessed plot, this earth
> This realm, this England.

It was about then that I saw I was headed for a landing in front of onrushing cars and on the unforgiving concrete of our nation's highway

149

system. I remembered from my brief instruction that there was a sewn hole in the parachute about the size of a basketball and if I managed to swivel it frontwards I'd speed forward in that direction. That did the trick and I floated over the interstate and at 16 miles per hour drifted toward the back yard of a house like a *deus ex machina*, terrifying a dog who ran around in harried circles underneath me before deciding to cower under the porch. I hit hard and rolled and collected the linens of the parachute and carried it out to the street where the relieved owners of the skydiving outfit found me, healthy and grinning, and hurriedly got me into their car before the house owner could complain.

On our ride back to Fort Benjamin Harrison, my lawyer buddy said, "That was really stupid, what we just did." But I was happy about it because I was fixed on the idea of becoming a writer and had the foreshadowing of an anecdote I could one day relate.

When my novel *Hitler's Niece* was published in Australia, a book reviewer criticized my biographical fiction as a vaguely illicit, new-fangled notion, seemingly forgetting that fully ten of Shakespeare's plays were histories of real English royalty who lived more than one hundred years before his writing.

I took my cue from Shakespeare with my first published novel, about the real-life Dalton Gang that was wiped out in Coffeyville, Kansas in 1892. I then explored biographical fiction further with *The Assassination of Jesse James by the Coward Robert Ford, Exiles*, about Gerard Manley Hopkins and his "Wreck of the Deutschland," *A Wild Surge of Guilty Passion*, and most recently *The Kid*, about William H. Bonney and his short, violent life in New Mexico.

I was on the staff of the Bread Loaf Writers' Conference in Vermont when I gave a reading from my work-in-progress, *The Assassination of Jesse James by the Coward Robert Ford*, specifically the last eight pages of Chapter 5 in which Bob Ford killed his idol Jesse on the morning of April 3rd, 1882. After the reading a friend came up to congratulate me on finishing the novel. But in fact it wasn't finished, for the model for its structure was based on Shakespeare's *Julius Caesar*, in which the Roman emperor is killed by Brutus and his allies in Act Three of a five-act play. My idea at the start was Jesse as Caesar, his wife Zee as Calpurnia, and the brothers Charley and Bob Ford in the assassin roles of Cassius and Brutus. And

I couldn't imagine the novel without "Part 3: Americana," a ninety-page section that dealt with the aftermath of Jesse's government-inspired assassination that in 1882 saw Bob Ford treated as a celebrity and hero but then over the years saw his fortunes change as the American people began to revile him. The famous folk song perhaps written by a minstrel named Billy Gashade "on the moment he heard the news," as one lyric claims, reflected the altered attitudes, for in "The Ballad of Jesse James" Robert Ford was called "that dirty little coward that shot Mr. Howard." And when Edward O'Kelly killed Bob with two blasts of a shotgun in 1892, he clearly thought he was carrying out a heroic act of revenge. And the public was behind him.

You may remember Paul Harvey on the radio, giving background on a celebrity we thought we knew, but then going a little farther as he told about a hidden life that was often dark but was shockingly illuminating about the figure's authentic personality. And with a smug, self-satisfied voice, Paul Harvey would confide, "And that's the *rest* of the story."

The rest of the story is what initially drew me to Robert Ford, and to all the other biographical novels I have written.

One of my favorite scenes in *Hamlet, Prince of Denmark* occurs in Act Three. Claudius has connived with Queen Gertrude to murder his brother, the king, not only usurping the crown but taking his wife. At one point he kneels in prayer and the late king's son sees him, and though he wants to kill King Claudius Hamlet hesitates for he worries that Claudius, murdered in the midst of prayer, could ascend to Heaven and not his rightful place in Hell, and so Hamlet exits. Another playwright may have thought that enough, but Shakespeare lets us into Claudius's mind as we hear that he is praying not for forgiveness for his rank offense but hoping that he will get away with his crime. And we have a flash of sympathy for the villain when, after Hamlet departs, he admits his prayers have been invalid as he is without remorse: "My words fly up," he says, "my thoughts remain below: Words without thoughts never to heaven go."

Shakespeare gives voices to his villains, letting Claudius, Iago, the Merchant of Venice, and the gleeful, dissembling Richard the Third explain themselves in a way that is familiar to us and in a self-reflective way that almost makes us like them. Richard, Duke of Gloucester, is determined to become king, and frankly admits to the audience that he's a liar who misquotes and misuses scripture, convincing the public that God bids them do evil rather than good. "And thus I clothe my naked villainy," Richard says, "with odd old ends stolen out of Holy Writ; and seem the saint, when most I play the devil."

My screwball comedy, *Isn't It Romantic?*—about the hijinks that follow the accident of a bickering French couple being waylaid in a small Nebraska town—was directly inspired by Shakespeare's fantasy *A Midsummer Night's Dream*, an inventive romantic comedy that, of all his plays, is the most frequently performed by schools and companies of amateurs. I was imitating the madcap films of Preston Sturges with my novel, but hovering over it, too, was Shakespeare. In fact, I went through each line of his play to find nifty phrasings I could steal and scatter throughout my pages like the cunningly hidden chocolates of Easter hunts. The book is bestrewn with the Bard's voice.

I'm so steeped in Shakespeare that when Tobias Wolff asked why I despised politics, I quite naturally called up Sonnet 129 about lust, saying politics was "The expense of spirit in a waste of shame."

Accountants of language have tallied a vocabulary of 17,677 words in Shakespeare's plays, sonnets, and narrative poems. And of those words, Shakespeare is credited with the invention of a stunning 1,700. Hence, one out of ten words he wrote in those pre-dictionary days were uniquely his own, though they may have been in England's common parlance. His neologisms and odd pairings are a significant part of his appeal.

I recall some critic saying that Macbeth was not in love with Lady Macbeth; rather he was in love with his wife's madness. Much of that infected my true crime novel, *A Wild Surge of Guilty Passion*, about a married corset salesman named Judd Gray who fell into a love affair with the beautiful, fun-loving, manipulating, and crazy Ruth Snyder, who convinced Judd to murder her husband Albert. In 1927, when the court trial occurred, it was considered the crime of the century and was covered by a dozen newspapers, including crafty reportage by Damon Runyon and Mae West—whom Ruth Snyder somewhat resembled. James M. Cain based his novel *Double Indemnity* on the same murder case, but his main protagonist agrees to kill the husband within the first seven pages of the novel, while for Judd Gray it was less an immediate decision than a kind of slow surrender halfway brought on by an excessive consumption of alcohol. It seemed to me a chronicle that Shakespeare would have been drawn to and so I felt required to undertake it.

Even in my novel about the outlaw William Henry McCarty whom we know as Billy the Kid, Shakespeare is in the wings. The Kid fell in love with the theatrical Sallie Chisum, niece of cattle baron John Chisum, and on a moonlight stroll with her, when he's failed to excite her interest, what else was there to do but quote Shakespeare's, "We are such stuff as dreams are made on, and our little life is rounded with a sleep."

"So you're going to bed now?" Billy asks.

"That's what I was implying, yes."

Billy just watched Sallie walk back to the house alone, thinking, *Could've said you love her, Kid.*

Months later Sallie sees the Kid again after he's magnificently risked death in a gun battle and she tells him he's "so adult now, so brazen, so something-or-other. I feel like I'm meeting you for the first time."

And later that night after dinner, she asks the Kid to join her on the veranda. I'll quote: "She seemed about to comment on the flashing riot of stars overhead but instead inquired if the Kid had read William Shakespeare's *Twelfth Night.*

"Of course not," he said. Weeks ago, he thought, he would have self-consciously lied that he had.

She said, "There's a line sung to a girl: 'Journeys end in lovers' meeting.' Which I feel has happened here. With us. And then: 'What is love? Tis not hereafter. *Present* mirth hath present laughter. What's to come is still unsure. In delay there lies no plenty, then come kiss me, Sweet-and-twenty. Youth's a stuff will not endure.'"

"You're the Sweet-and-twenty?" Billy asks.

"Aren't you the clever one," she says.

"And I agree with that last part about youth," Billy says. "Ain't everlasting."

What seems to be everlasting is Shakespeare.

Actor Ben Kingsley has said, "Performing Shakespeare is a lot like galloping on a horse you love at full speed. If the horse feels insecure with you on its back it will throw you and break your neck. You will lose your voice, your lines, and you won't know how to breathe. But in the end it will be absolutely thrilling."

And that's what draws me to Shakespeare again and again. There's a thrill to his writing that I want to incorporate in my own.

# SUNDAY DRIVES

## Alan Boye's *Complete Roadside Guide to Nebraska*

WE ARE TALKING ABOUT HIGHWAYS HERE—HILLY, SLOW, TWO-LANE blacktops with fall leaves flowing across them, home to roadside attractions and tractors with hoisted plows and hidden old drivers with both hands on the wheel of a car that will soon be on blocks—not interstate 80 and that flat, hard-driving stretch of the Great Plains between Kearney and Ogallala where the few radio stations peter out, the weather is either too hot or too cold, and even people who ought to know better find themselves thinking, *Why would anyone choose to live here?*

You tell friends in the East you're from Nebraska and you get these looks, like you'd used a spoon to chip your way out through the floor of a prison in China. But then it turns out that the only Nebraska those friends have seen is from behind a parade of semis in the hell of July, a green blur of cottonwoods hiding the Platte and heat waves shimmying the farmhouses and silos in the distance as the travelers floorboarded it to get to Omaha or Denver. Whereas those of us who love Nebraska probably first learned about it on highways on hunting trips or family visits or old-fashioned Sunday afternoon outings to no place in particular.

The fifties were full of such jaunts for me. We'd go to church and my brother, Rob, and I would lie on the floor to look at the comics in the Omaha *World-Herald* that weren't too hard for us while Mom cooked a full noon dinner of red potatoes and gravy and green peas and soft-as-butter roast beef. And then we'd watch television for an hour or so until we all got bored with it and Dad asked, "You want to go for a ride?"

My father drove, of course, my mother sat with him in the front, and Rob and I stared out our own windows in the back of a black, four-door, 1950 Plymouth that is still my favorite car. We'd head west from Omaha on highway 6, but Dad would turn north or south according to fancy, halting for a yard sale in Wahoo that seemed interesting or for a truck gardener's market basket of corn outside Blair. We'd visit shirttail relatives in Pender who were two old bachelors and their sister and hear how the harvest was as we ate a fresh cherry pie that seemed to be heating in the oven on the off chance that city folk happened by. I have a memory of us shamelessly heading up to a farmhouse near West Point in order to get four glasses of water and of the farmer being so happy to have our company that it was tough politics to get away before nightfall.

We mostly just stared out the Plymouth's windows with the faint puzzlement and irritation of people who can't read, seeing bleak cemeteries of tilted gravestones, sudden creeks unnamed on our map, and grand old buildings that hid their histories like pearl necklaces under a hand-me-down coat. We depended upon serendipity for the success of those weekend trips, and often our discoveries were so few that Rob and I fell asleep to the hum of the tires.

If the Hansen family had owned Alan Boye's *Complete Roadside Guide to Nebraska* in the fifties we would have found more wonders and surprises than we did, for if Alan Boye has proved anything it's that the Cornhusker state is full of marvels far greater than its football team—formerly called, he tells us, the Rattlesnake Boys and the Bugeaters—and that there's more to Nebraska than first hits the eye.

You find out here that the town of Weeping Water gets its poetic name from the French *L'Eau qui Pleure,* which in turn was a mistranslation of the Otoe for water running over a falls; that the Republican River near Alma was once known by a scatological name because of the huge buffalo herds that filled it with their manure; and that Loup City, the Polish Capital of Nebraska, gets its name from a fur trapper's French term for a famous wolf that roamed the river banks.

Without this guide the highway traveler would be hard put to guess that the True Value Hardware store in Falls City was once the Gehling Opera House, that Plattsmouth was home to cigar factories, that Glurs Tavern in Columbus is the oldest saloon west of the Missouri River, that

Lincoln was the origin of the Frisbee, Lawrence Welk's champagne music, and my college friend, *Cliff Notes*, or that it was in DeWitt in 1929 that the Vise-Grip wrench was invented—"a tool so useful, some say, that the object it is used on will often lose its usefulness."

Even the names of places conjure up the irony, misery, and violence of our nineteenth-century past—Devil's Nest, Dismal River, Dogtown, Dumbell Ranch, Massacre Canyon, Rawhide Creek, Robber's Cave, Whisky Run—but Alan Boye here provides the history that few of the residents know. (When will the locals finally forget that their town of Herman was named for a railway conductor? Are there people now in Cody who think it was named for Buffalo Bill?) And Alan Boye gives us thumbnail biographies and tales of the famous—Willa Cather, Black Elk, Wild Bill Hickok, Mari Sandoz—as well as those who ought to be—Antonine Barada, Doc "Evil Spirit of the Plains" Carver, Iron Eyes, J. Sterling Morton, Madam Anna Wilson.

Unidentified flying objects seem to have a fascination with Nebraska, for there have been sightings of foreign machinery in the sky as long ago as 1884 in Max—my favorite account—and 1897 in Omaha and Inavale; and no less than ten towns, from Sidney to Bellevue, seem to have been inspected by "elliptical," "hovering," "glowing" objects "as large as a hangar" in the twentieth century.

Children's highway games could be made of the questions often asked throughout these pages, or invented from information included inside: Taylor, on US Highway 183, has seen its population increase by just two between the years 1930 and 1980. At that rate, it will be 7490 before Taylor's population achieves five hundred. What, therefore, is Taylor's present population? And how many know the titles of our eight roadside sculptures? ("Arrival," "Crossing the Plains," "Erma's Desire," "Nebraska Gateway," "Nebraska Wind Sculpture," "Over/Under," "Praxis," "Roadway Confluence.")

This is irresistible reading, a book browser's delight, full of affections, oddments, trivia, well-informed opinions—Nebraska's prettiest small town is Peru, its most underrated novelist Wright Morris, its greatest philosopher John G. Neihardt, its meanest reputation, the town of Arnold—and full, too, of the kinds of funny and frightening things that my mother might have read aloud in the car as we waited at a railroad crossing for the Burlington freight train to clank past. *The Complete Roadside Guide to Nebraska* would have been a book impossible to write were it not, for Alan Boye, so obviously a labor of love. Readers of this wonderful second edition may well find that his passion has become theirs.

V

# WHY THE WEST?

WHY DOES BIG SKY COUNTRY LIFT MY SPIRITS?
Why is it that the British automobile manufacturer Rover named its high-end model a Range Rover? And why are GMC SUVS named after the Alaskan wilderness?

Why were Rob and I given cowboy boots for our third birthday? And why did we refuse to take them off?

Why is it that more people jump off the Golden Gate Bridge in San Francisco than the Brooklyn Bridge that spans the East River?

Why is it that the cigarette named after the Duke of Marlborough, an English lord, was famously advertised by a cowboy?

Why is the American director John Ford, born in Cape Elizabeth, Maine, principally known for Westerns, though they constitute less than one-third of his films?

Why did my grandfather, who grew up in Spain, work as a hired hand in Iowa and finally ranch in Colorado?

Why was the bunkhouse that could house twelve hands still there some thirty years after it was needed?

Why does Fort Huachuca, Arizona, have the greatest horse population in the Army?

Why does the English artist David Hockney consider a major influence on his work the Laurel & Hardy films shot in Los Angeles?

Why are seven of the ten most populated cities in the United States located west of the Mississippi? And why can so few name all of them?

Why do so many Americans feel their country is overpopulated when 96 percent is parkland and open range?

Why do interstate truckers so often wear Western hats and boots?

Why are there still rodeos when so few of the skills on example are still practiced?

Why do I grin when my car radio can find no signals somewhere west of Ogallala, Nebraska?

Why are the riveted blue jeans that Levi Strauss began manufacturing in California in 1873 still, after all these years, in fashion?

Why are the Western comics starring Lucky Luke and the Dalton gang still a hit in France?

Why are Karl May's books about the American West still huge bestsellers in Germany more than ninety years after his death? And why did he never visit the region he wrote about?

Why do movie characters on the run almost always head west?

Why is prostitution legal in Nevada and nowhere else?

Why do cowboy poetry festivals attract greater audiences than the other kind?

Why did the Italian soldier in Rome insist on reciting the names of thirty-two Indian tribes?

Why did so many nineteenth-century artists who visited the West end up painting imaginary landscapes?

Why did John Wayne inherit his nickname, Duke, from a horse?

Why, in college, did I go out into the Omaha countryside at night and just stand in the fall fields, inhaling the healing air?

# THE LAND THAT TIME FORGOT

I FIRST THINK OF THE WEATHER. STUNNINGLY HOT SUMMER DAYS, THE July sun a furnace, grasshoppers chirring in the fields of alfalfa, and nothing moving, no one but me fool enough to be out, the shimmer of heat waves warping the farmhouse in the distance, and the asphalt road beneath my sneakers softening into tar. Or January and its zero cold stiffening my face on my predawn paper route, my gloves and galoshes not enough to protect fingers and toes that hurt as if hammered, and a fierce snow flying with the sting of pins as I slog forward through high drifts, twelve years old and near tears.

The hottest temperature ever recorded in Nebraska was 118 degrees, and the coldest, –47. And there's a wide range of climate even within the state, with flooding possible in the southeast while the parched west worries through weeks of drought. Our thunderstorms are the stuff of horror movies: lashing rain and a far-off flash of light in the heavens, then the scratchy sound of sailcloth tearing until the fifty-megaton bomb goes off and children scream all over the neighborhood.

Also, of course, there are tornadoes, more than two thousand of them in the last fifty years. Once an Omaha friend driving home from his office noticed the May afternoon becoming strangely cool and gloomy and he glanced into his rearview mirror. His initial impression was of a sepia cloud and the churning turmoil of hundreds of crows. And then he realized he was seeing the swaying funnel of a tornado and what he saw flying around in the whirlwind were not crows but, as he gently put it to me, "things." I have read aftermath articles about horses in flight, about straw pounded through planks like ten-penny nails, about a dead woman found sitting stiffly upright in her front porch rocker but a mile away from home, about a house destroyed except for the dining room wall with its ornately framed print of Leonardo da Vinci's *Last Supper*.

Nebraska, meaning "Flat Water," was a Plains Indian name for the swift, shallow, brown Platte River that streams eastward the length of the state, sistering what is now Interstate 80. The first settlers used to lament that the Platte was "too thin to plow and too thick to drink." Locals still maintain it's "a mile wide and an inch deep," and Mark Twain claimed the Platte would only become a respectable river if it were laid on its side. The geography that the Platte slides through was part of what was once called "the Great American Desert" when the Nebraska Territory included all the states between the Missouri River and the Rocky Mountains and from the fortieth parallel of southern Kansas northward to the Canadian border. When Nebraska became the thirty-seventh state in 1867, it was scaled down in size, but its area of seventy-seven thousand square miles is still gigantic by eastern standards, large enough to contain all of New England plus New Jersey. Wayfarers on the Oregon Trail who got through the wide emptiness used to congratulate themselves by saying, "I have seen the elephant."

A hundred years ago a Nebraska geologist maintained "Rainfall follows the plow," and it's a fact that once European immigrants with nothing more to lose began cultivating the prairie of Nebraska, the Sudan of the first explorers gave way to some of America's richest farmland: waving acres of corn, wheat, sorghum, soybeans, and sugar beets, or sandhill grasslands where most of the state's six million cattle feed. Hidden underneath that land is the Ogallala Aquifer, a huge underground reservoir roughly the size of California that was formed by geologic action eons ago. Wells needed to reach into the earth no more than fifty feet before they tapped into a pure water source that seemed everlasting. Windmills and irrigation have made such use of that great lake that now, with an annual farm income of six billion dollars, Nebraska trails only California and Texas in agricultural prosperity.

And it's rural in the extreme: only Alaska has less land devoted to metropolitan areas. So there's still a great vacancy in the dunes northwest of Kearney, with less than seven people per square mile. (Omaha, for example, has one hundred fifty.) Which means in half the state you have six-man football teams, volunteer fire departments, houses that are un-locked, two or more grades conjoined in the schools, weeklies that list the wedding presents the happy couple received, five hundred-watt radio sta-tions whose way of giving the news is to read aloud the front page. There the hired hands still ride horses. Some roads are scarcely more than Cat-erpillared cattle trails. Houses are starkly exposed on the topography, as in a painting by Edward Hopper. Rarely is there landscaping: with so much potential for loneliness, privacy is not a high priority. There you know the names and kin and histories of everyone you see. Once my brother-in-law surprised the sunrise occupants of a sandhills diner by wandering in and sitting alone at a booth. While he scanned the breakfast menu he could feel the men in feed caps and bib overalls staring at him until one finally strolled over and said, "We all want to know who you are and why you're here." No fear or warning was involved; it was sheer curiosity.

Ethnically, the heritage is primarily German, then Irish, then Scan-dinavian and English. In a population of one million seven hundred thou-sand—Philadelphia has as many people—only a little over five percent are Hispanic, four percent are African-American, one percent Asian, less than one percent American Indian. I was in high school when I first sam-pled Mexican food or had a Chinese dish that was not chop suey. I was ten years old when I first saw a Jew, a red-haired kid at a bowling alley, wearing jeans, a cowboy shirt, and a knitted yarmulke. A friend once insisted his town of sixteen thousand was not as insulated as some outsiders thought, declaring, "We even have a black family now."

Up-to-date as the state sometimes strives to be, there's still a land-that-time-forgot quality to much if it. I once drove through a small town on the 4th of July and felt I had happened onto some Disneyland version of an America long gone: a white gazebo in the main square; girls in shorts writing their names in the twilight with sparklers; the old folks licking ice cream cones; a purple-costumed marching band just finished playing and the haggard members sitting on the street curbs, hugging their instru-ments, their high hats off, eating hot dogs and sipping Coca Cola through straws; a grinning boy racing his Schwinn beside my car with an American flag flying from his red rear fender and balloons tied against his spokes in order to make a blatting, motorcycle noise. It could have been a movie set for Thornton Wilder's *Our Town*.

Middle American normalcy is still the main draw. Whenever I have asked people why they moved here from the east or west coast, their initial reply is virtually always, "Well, it's a great place to raise kids." At last look Nebraska was number one in job growth, increasing 2.6 percent while the nation as a whole declined. Wages are low—the state ranks forty-fifth in teacher salaries—but so is the cost of living. A full breakfast at Cecil's is $3.70. And reading real estate ads can be hallucinatory to those who've just moseyed in from overpriced regions: 12 rm mansion, $300k. Small wonder realtors claim Nebraska has the highest percentage of home ownership in the nation. It also has America's cheapest coal and, thanks to a mixture of corn-derived ethanol, startlingly inexpensive gasoline. But the telling statistics have to do with the concerns of families. Ranked sixth among the fifty states in "livability," Nebraska is twelfth in books per capita, seventh in public libraries, fourth in community hospitals, third in percentage of government expenditures going to education, and first in the public high school graduation rate at 91.9 percent. Nebraska's students score one hundred points higher than the national average on the Scholastic Aptitude Test. And if they stay put, they tend to achieve senescence in Nebraska, which is ranked fifth in the percentage of the population older than eighty-five. (The snide may recall singer and sausage-maker Jimmy Dean's comment on those who forsook worldly pleasures for a more healthy lifestyle: "You may not live to be a hundred but it'll feel like it.")

The old can-do spirit is alive and well here. With no available wood or stone for housing, the pioneers chopped blocks of sod and called it marble, heated and cooked with cow manure and called it Nebraska coal. In civic response to the area's treelessness, Nebraskans sowed fast-growing, fast-spreading cottonwoods, invented the spring rite of Arbor Day, created near Thedford America's largest hand-planted timberland, and achieved in Omaha the Lied Jungle, the world's largest indoor rainforest. Cyclical flooding losses have been curtailed by the most extensive system of flood mitigation projects in the country. The architectural wonder of its gorgeous state capitol building was paid for as it was constructed, without the aid of bonds or sales and income taxes, levies that were still a generation off.

South of Omaha is Offutt Air Force Base, home of the United States Strategic Command, the national control center for the Navy's submarine

launched Polaris missiles, the Air Force's bombers, and the interconti-
nental ballistic missiles hidden in silos, as well as "warfighter" space operations, warning systems, intelligence assessments, and global strategic
planning. Arguably the most significant military installation in the world
and the subject of great wrangling in Congress and among the military
services, Offutt has managed to maintain a strikingly low profile in the
community, hardly a word of it in the nightly news. This is no Fort Ben-
ning or Cape Canaveral; it's the picture of laconic restraint and muscular,
just-doing-my-job-ma'am dutifulness that perfectly correlates to the personality of its home state.

Characteristic of Nebraskans are sincerity, independence, friendli-
ness, stoicism, piety, and caution. Conservative values are predominant,
good citizenship is honored; the Armed Forces have no problem recruit-
ing. The percentage of registered voters is twelve points higher than the
U.S. norm. Independent Republican George W. Norris, who represented
Nebraska in Congress for forty years, promoted the state's one-house,
unicameral legislature, and because of that Nebraska ranks last in the nation in its number of state politicians. I have never met anyone who did
not consider that a good thing. Although the statewide vote generally tilts
Republican in presidential elections, there's a surprising disinclination to
vote along party lines—the state legislature is at least nominally nonpar-
tisan—and there's even a contradictory, nuisance tendency to split the
vote, with a governor of one party and a lieutenant governor or attorney
general of the opposition.

Owing to its position on the map—it's slightly north of the geo-
graphical center of the nation—Nebraska commands attention in a way
that more outlying states do not. But the general notion seems to be that
it's a dull, deadly, *Children of the Corn* kind of place, each steely-eyed and
taciturn face concealing a fiend with a rifle. Theodore Sorensen, the head
speechwriter for President Kennedy, once dismissed his home state as "a
place to get away from and a place to die." Even those who have not gotten
away sometimes convey the same impression. Omaha is the mecca of the
state, the flourishing, hilly, spottily cosmopolitan city where people hon-
eymoon, have their larks, celebrate high school graduation, and find jobs
or objects they can't get elsewhere; yet there's a bumper sticker that reads:
"Omaha—Where the West begins and the East just sort of peters out."

And when the *Omaha World-Herald* ran an article about the local ballet troupe, its headline was: "NYC DANCER FINDS OMAHA AS GOOD A PLACE AS ANY." The idea for many is to never single yourself out or get too big for your britches, but to accept your measliness and stolidly accomplish your chores.

The grand exception to that is the majesty of Big Red football. Since 1970 the University of Nebraska varsity has won five national championships, and in the years 1993 to 1997 the football team won sixty times, including three unbeaten and untied seasons, for the finest five-year record in NCAA history. Memorial Stadium in Lincoln, which can accommodate over eighty thousand fans, making it Nebraska's third-largest city, has had 255 consecutive sell-outs, another NCAA record. And the list goes on. City streets can be without traffic when a game is played. Elderly women in retirement homes are rooted in front of television sets. Red jerseys, jackets, seat cushions, memorabilia, and the other stuff of fandom are everywhere, no matter the season. Nebraska football is not just the primary feature of sports pages, not just the common religion and language of the state, but the overriding id of the psyche. I have seen people who never even thought of higher education become sick with desolation when the university's football team loses, wild with exaltation when they win.

Still, when I think of Nebraska I first think of its climate and wide, blond cornfields, the green windbreaks that shield a farmhouse, windmill, and barn, skies that are blue as a jay. Sixty percent of its days are sunny. Well above average. And each season has its intimations of paradise. Cloudless October days when it's just cool enough to hint a sweater, giant harvesters rolling through the fields of sorghum while the operator tunes his Walkman to the Cornhusker football game. Or the first soft snow of December, the elm tree branches being mittened in white and the flakes hanging above you like God just shook the paperweight. Warming afternoons in March, shrubs burgeoning pinkly with their new buds, water quietly trickling beneath the final holdouts of ice, a baseball smacking a glove somewhere. August nights when the twirling sprinklers have made their crawl of the yard and the pale moon is rising, but it's just so pleasant out it's a shame to go inside, and the sultry air is sweet with the tang of mown bluegrass, a smell that seems to heal the lungs with each inhalation.

# HALCYON DAYS

IN 1977, I WAS IN ILLINOIS SELLING COLLEGE TEXTBOOKS FOR RANDOM House by day and writing fiction in motel rooms at night when I learned I'd been awarded a Wallace E. Stegner creative writing fellowship at Stanford. Elated doesn't begin to describe the feelings of confirmation and anticipation I enjoyed for the next few months. The fellowship then was only worth $4,500 in total so I was really poor, owned no car, and went everywhere on a bike or on the bus. But in the fall I managed to win a $1,000 prize in the *Penthouse* New Writers Short Story Contest and also sold a short story to *The Atlantic Monthly*, and that income meant more to me then than a paperback sale does to me now.

Our fiction writing classes met around a long conference table in the second-story Jones Room. My classmates were, alphabetically Peter Fish, David Hellerstein, Tom McNeal, James Thomas, and Susan Welch. Peter was a Mirilees Fellow, that is, he was working on a Master of Arts degree. We others weren't. Peter had graduated from Yale and then served an internship with *Mademoiselle* magazine; he became a senior editor at *Sunset*. David Hellerstein was primarily a medical school student at Stanford, but he took the fiction workshop to keep his sanity and he eventually became a psychiatrist. Tom McNeal had earned his Master of Fine Arts in fiction writing at the University of California-Irvine's prestigious program and taught high school for a year in Hay Springs, Nebraska, a job that some years later would inform his novel *Goodnight, Nebraska*, the movie *Tully* that was based on one of his short stories, and the bestselling novel *To Be Sung Underwater*. James Thomas was a PhD candidate at the University of Utah who'd recently sold the story "Paco and I at Sea" to *Esquire*. That story would become part of his collection *Pictures, Moving* (1985). And, finally, Susan Welch was a journalist and book review editor for the Minneapolis *Tribune*. She, too, was working on short stories. In fact, I was the only one of us working on a novel then, having completed about half of *Desperadoes*—a historical novel on the Dalton gang in nineteenth century Kansas and Oklahoma—before I got to Stanford.

The pattern for our fiction writing workshops was that one or a couple of us would volunteer to submit some pages on a future date and make multiple copies, handing the pages out to each of us on the class before we were due to have our fiction discussed. We each served as each other's editors in this way, and the class was spent in praising, justifying, criticizing, or recommending other solutions for elements of the manuscript. I suspect I was the most aggressive in noting my comments and urgings of change. Susan confined her comments to long, kind, summary letters. Tom made faint pencil marks in the margins indicating good things with a "+" and not-so-good with a "–."

Our first workshop instructor was Richard Scowcroft, the jolly chair of the English Department, who had the good grace not to object when I submitted a grossly overlong manuscript when my chance at a workshop session came up. He seemed somewhat puzzled by my project's combination of the Western, the literary, and the historical but the overall response to my writing was very positive and I felt encouraged to go on. In the second quarter poet and novelist John L'Heureux, the director of the creative writing program, took over our workshops. As it happened, he'd been a fiction editor at *The Atlantic Monthly* in 1970 and sent me a very kind letter in rejecting one of my stories, so we were simpatico from the first and I can still recall my overwhelming cheer and delight when he read almost all of the novel and predicted, "The first editor who sees this is going to buy it."

There was a wild party for my thirtieth birthday that December and as I closed my eyes to make a wish before blowing out the birthday candles on the cake, my friend Tobias Wolff wisecracked, "Well, there goes the Nobel Prize." I have no memory of what I wished then, but it probably had a good deal to do with *Desperadoes*, and that wish was in short order answered when my agent called from New York one rainy Monday evening in February and said, "You're awfully hard to get ahold of when there's good news." She'd gotten the typescript of the novel to Robert Gottlieb at Alfred A. Knopf on Friday, he'd read it over the weekend, and told her he wanted it that Monday morning.

John L'Heureux and I were supposed to go out for dinner that evening, but there were so many people I wanted to tell about the sale—my family, my former teacher John Irving, other friends—that I only ended up going out for some festive drinks with a girlfriend later that night. It was then I learned that Toby Wolff had accepted a teaching job at Arizona State University, and I presumed I would replace him as one of the three Jones Lecturers in fiction writing. So I had some sense of stability and income after many up and down years. The next day I bought an answering machine so I'd never again miss an agent's call, and a month or so later bought an old, ramshackle Volkswagen so I would not be so dependent on others.

Our spring quarter instructor was the nineteenth-century scholar Albert Guerard who graciously allowed our classes to meet in his grand French house on campus and served us wine and appetizers as we jawed about the fiction. Harriet Doerr, a widow in her seventies, had joined our fiction writing group by then and was submitting chapters of the glorious novel that would become *Stones for Ibarra* (1984).

*Desperadoes* was published to pretty nice critical acclaim in 1979. I was teaching "Narration" and "Advanced Fiction Writing" to undergraduates at Stanford as a Jones Lecturer then and would continue on with the lectureship's three-year term until I left to become a member of the University of Michigan's Society of Fellows in 1981. Occasionally, I would sit in on other workshops—I recall submitting my story "Playland" to a class Robert Stone was teaching—and in that way I became friends with Stephanie Vaughn and Michael Koch whom I'd later join on the faculty at Cornell University. Michael is now the managing editor of *Epoch*, a quarterly where I've frequently published my fiction.

I have since gone back to Stanford to teach a quarter-long course on the novella as part of the Isaac Stein Visiting Writer program, and I often make it up there for dinner parties or readings. Some of the Stanford friends I made in 1977 and after are still friends I see regularly today. We all, I think, look back on our days as Stegners with greater gratitude than nostalgia, for that year for me is not one I yearn to return to but one that helped enormously in getting me to where I am now.

# BAD WEATHER GOLF

April in Omaha. The skies were bleak and forbidding at sunrise, but I still harried my twin brother, Rob, into our first golf outing of the year. When we got to Elmwood Park, a hard rain was pelting down, the drops as fat and cold as chilled grapes. Hunching under a scolding wind as we hurried into the pro shop, Rob reasonably proposed calling the whole thing off, but I was hankering for a game and was not about to let foul weather get in the way. I even harangued Rob into paying our greens fees to a cashier in the pro shop, who smirked when he said, "Tee's open."

Rob zipped on his rain suit and sighed at me, as is his wont, but I just strode forward like a hearty lad greeting a grand adventure. We teed off, Rob's foozled drive sizzling through the high soaked grass and then stalling, my own shot trickily squirting off the wet clubface and onto a soft and shamrock-green fairway for all of 100 yards. Walking to my gleaming white ball, my fingers already stiffening, rain pattering noisily on my hat, I saw a Plymouth Valiant veer off to the side of a tarmac road that winds between the first green and the second tee, and from it debouched a man in a trench coat, screwing the lens on a fancy camera. His head shaking from side to side with disbelief, he introduced himself as a newspaper photographer whose editor had sent him, he thought in vain, "to find out if there was anybody crazy enough to play golf in weather like this."

*C'est moi.*

My brother gave me a frosty look, his fears for my mental health confirmed. But there, indeed, on the front page of the next morning's *Omaha World Herald* was a handsome, full-color photo of Rob and me, head down and dauntless, trudging through a gale of the kind that tilts sailors at the helm.

And you wonder why you're not famous.

The fact is, when I took up golf again after giving it up in frustration for fifteen years, I got hooked on the game so completely that I found it impossible to quit just because of foul weather. It seemed unsporting and unmanly; it was like you couldn't take a joshing. Even on the fourth hole of only my second round, when a hostile Iowa rain was causing wiser golfers to flee for the Hawkeye clubhouse, I persuaded my chilly playing partner to put up with it for a little longer. Holding out my hand in the wet, I told him the rain was already letting up, and fully believed it myself. Clouds were not looming blackly in the horizon; they were shredding apart, heading elsewhere. Why, the very turbulence in the tossing trees meant the front was passing through. And so we trudged on through a full eighteen holes, thoroughly drenched by the ninth, our feet squishing in our shoes, our clothes weighing all of forty pounds, our flailing shots shanking into the woods or spritzing weakly along the fairways with tall rooster tails of water spray in their wake. And though my friend chided me about my fraudulent meteorology, and our scores soared higher than our IQs, it was golf, by gosh, and I loved it.

It's a fixation that's often misunderstood. I recall, for example, an autumn drizzle that was like the fine spray that floats from a car wash—just annoying enough to prevent my playing a round, but not so forbidding that I passed up the chance to practice on the driving range. To my glad astonishment another guy was out there, about five stalls away, tinkering with his takeaway, adjusting his hand position at the top, pausing now and then to dry the grips on his irons with a towel he fastidiously folded inside his bag. We offered each other formal nods of recognition, not unlike the kind in the gentlemen's clubs of P. G. Wodehouse's fiction. And then we set to the perfection of our swings.

I found out that after fifteen minutes a fine drizzle is indistinguishable from a full rain. My clothes were cold and sagging, my hands were red and raw, and my hair was enameled to my head, and as I paused to consider just leaving a half basket of range balls to my new friend five stalls down, a workman zipping by on the street rolled down his pickup's window to yell, "You guys are nuts!"

My range mate looked at me with the flush of embarrassment, *Sorry for that unpleasantness, old chap,* and then went back to his golf mechanics. But I was fatally inhibited by the charge. If I was confident of my own unnuttiness, I was not so certain of his, and as he finicked obsessively with the faulty clenching of his fingers on the grip of a fairway wood, he seemed mad indeed, and I held up my half basket of balls and called to him, "You can have these!" Engrossed in his reclamation project, he simply grunted and I hurried away.

Rain, you'll have noticed, changes to snow in the cold. Winter is a tougher challenge for the zealous golfer. I taught in the English department at Cornell University one year and had a wonderful time in September and October playing nine holes a few times a week after I finished my afternoon classes. But just when New York's fall foliage was reaching chromatic splendor and the fairways were green as Irish loam, a faculty colleague flicked his ball out of the ninth hole's cup with his putter and flatly said, "Well, that's probably our last round for the year."

I was shocked that he could be so sanguine about it, but indeed he was right. Cold, blustering winds and rain soon gave way to snow and more snow, and the fairways became trails for heavily bundled cross-country skiers. Watching golf on TV and reading the reporting of the inestimable Herbert Warren Wind was not enough to quell my wish to play, so I would go out to Ithaca's public course and peel off my hunting coat and gloves just long enough to hit a few tee shots into the 18th fairway. As I hurriedly dressed again and fetched my fluorescent orange shag bag of balls from a half-foot of snow, I found twenty or more other deep holes in the powder, as if a javelin had been hurled repeatedly from a great distance, but at the terminus of each crystalline tunnel were brand new Titleist balls that an equally impatient head pro must have launched out there. I felt the joy of the truly insane, who finally find a loony affirmation in the weirdness of another. You are not alone!

I hit the links often that winter in Ithaca, inventing my own version of cold weather rules wherein fantastic bounces off the ice could be replayed and any golf ball near the frozen green was presumed holed in two putts. One fine Sunday, when the temperature was flirting with the 30s, when the sky was a periwinkle blue, and here and there fairway was emerging from the acres of whiteness like the humps of a herd of whales, I ventured onto a Cornell course tracked up by dog walkers and the trails of toboggans and cross-country skiers. And I was scoring pretty well, just two over par after the fifth hole, when I happened to look over my shoulder and saw far off in the distance a sheriff's car and the sheriff in his navy blue parka beside it, his hands on his hips, possibly yelling to me and most certainly deciding how far he was willing to walk to cite me for whatever misdemeanor he'd invent. I pretended obliviousness, a popular stance with criminals, right there behind just-fell-off-the-turnip-truck innocence. I finished the front nine in four o'clock darkness, my fingers stinging and the feeling pretty much gone from my face, and then I tramped back to the parking lot and found on my Mazda's front windshield an inked note that read, "The golf course is CLOSED!"

Good information, sheriff. Haul in those toboggans and dog walkers, too.

I hated winter in upstate New York enough to go elsewhere, finding a job professing English at the University of Arizona. And there, of course, the problem was summer. But I have a high tolerance for heat, the jam-packed courses of winter were practically vacant by May, and rounds were half-priced in the afternoons, so except for the heatstroke and dehydration—hardly worth mentioning really—the hot weather there seemed fairly felicitous.

But farther south in Cancun, Mexico, May weather can be foul indeed. Say you are baking at 450 degrees and you open the oven door for a peek at how the cherry cobbler is turning out. The heat that blasts your face like a foretaste of hell is Cancun in the summer.

High noon and 115 degrees, the feathering breeze as hot as a hair dryer, I got out of my rental car and found my shoes were sticking to the softened asphalt in the Club de Golf's parking lot. Crows stood in shadow with their beaks open, panting. Everything green seemed to sizzle. The head pro smiled at my fiery third-day-in-the-tropics sunburn and when I offered him the fee for a full round told me in Spanish to just try playing nine holes first. If I liked the course I could pay for the full eighteen at the turn.

Within a few holes I knew a full nine would hardly be possible. Quarts of sweat were trickling down my forearms and legs, and the heat was dizzying. The skies seemed as bleached as old denim, so I had a hard time following the flight of my ball, and when it hit it bounded wildly off line on fairways that were hard as terra-cotta tiles. Six over par after three holes, I hurried my backswing and got ahead of the ball on the fourth tee, blocking the ball far off to the right of the fourth fairway, into high weeds and darkness that I felt sure was home to a hundred kinds of poisonous crawling things. Accepting a one-stroke penalty for an unplayable lie, I then hooked my next shot far left of the green into jungle that was full of the cawing, ticking, screeing sounds of Tarzan films. I again took a stroke for an unplayable lie, in frustration pitched the next shot over the green, muffed my chip into the fluff of the collar, and three putted, for a nine. I was fairly certain golf used to be fun but couldn't just then recall why.

And yet I went on. Every now and then I would see a Mexican foursome genially playing far ahead on the 12th or 15th fairway and wonder, *How do they do handle the heat?* I felt I was slumping through a red-embered barbecue pit, that the Caribbean sun was full of malice for me alone, and that whatever water I found to drink was oozing immediately through my skin as if it were way too hot inside. And my scorecard looked like a preposterous fiction, for I was feebly lashing at the ball like a convict doing hard time with a sickle on an Alabama chain gang. Thoroughly sapped and wobbly by the ninth hole, I hit yet another wayward tee shot and lost the last ball in my bag. And with relief I told the course, "You win," and slouched to my car and my air-conditioned hotel. I stayed in Mexico for one more week and was not tempted to pick up the sticks again.

It's wind I have to contend with in California. I have a friend named John who often grouses that the wind never helps his shots. Which is a bit like saying that when you were a kid you used to walk five miles to school and it was uphill both ways.

The havoc of wind is the problem. The famous seaside seventh hole at Pebble Beach is a case in point. The heavily bunkered and downhill par three plays at 135 yards from the white tees. Yet the hardiest pros have had to use one irons when facing into a fierce headwind, and with a squall behind you even a wedge can fly the green. Even in the same foursome there can be such wild fluctuations in the force of the wind that the question, "What club d'ja use there?" can become pointless.

With honors on the seventh and with a pretty good zephyr behind me, I hit a hard sixty-degree wedge and watched the wind hold the ball up like a good waiter handling a food tray in heavy traffic, carrying it far over the flagstick before letting it wallop into the furthest edge of the wide bunker behind the green, a foot or so from a watery grave. My friend John was next and tried a soft sand wedge, but the wind seemed to disdain it, plunking his ball in the front bunker, fully 40 yards short of mine. "I thought you used a lob wedge," he said.

"I did," I said. "I'm real strong."

My favorite wind shot occurred at Spanish Bay just up the coast. I got too far ahead of my hands and blocked my drive far off to the right into a phalanx of sequoias that so shaded out the sun that there was nothing but a soft cushion of pine needles below my ball. My friend, who was safely in the fairway and knew the hole was worth four dollars in so-called skins, helpfully warned me not to make a bad situation worse but to take my medicine and chip out sideways. But I saw that there was a six-foot-wide alley through the trees, and 180 yards ahead was the faint right edge of the green, with the flagstick far to the left and back. At the time a 20-mile-per-hour wind was shuttling balls from right to left, so I set up with the intention of just hitting the ball through the alley, then hooded my four-iron clubface a little to the left to impart the counterclockwise spin that produces a draw or hook. *Hit through the ball*, I told myself. And what a sweet golf shot it was! Rising softly, my ball flew straight as a surveyor's string between the sequoias and then began working to the left as gently as a mother's hand combing her daughter's hair. At 100 yards the wind found it and teased it further left so that the ball struck the green pretty much in the middle, kicked left for two hops, and then the hook spin forced it to skitter further until it settled about five feet below the pin. I sank the putt for a birdie and $4.

Usually things do not go as well. Winds find a fade and turn it first into a slice, then into a one-stroke-and-loss-of-distance penalty. But I have fonder memories of an afternoon when a huge wind was blowing behind me on a tee box high above the hole at a 166-yard par three. I tried a hard nine-iron and watched the ball hang forever over the green, traveling further and further like a child who has run off with the circus, before it softly fell into the far-side rough and hid, easily 170 yards away. "Wow!" I said. "A nine iron. Did you see that?!"

The guy I was playing with seemed to fear this hacker thought he was a golfing immortal for he brought me to earth by saying, "You had a little help there."

At the next par three a hurricane was now firmly perpendicular to a flagstick that was tucked practically out of sight on the left behind a hill of scrub brush and just plain nothing. I hoped to find the right side of the green and let the wind shove the ball toward the hole, but I instead sliced it toward oblivion forty yards to the right. And while I watched, frustrated, hating my fault-ridden swing, the wind hauled the ball even farther than I thought it would, looping it back so that it seemed to be floating sideways, and fell to the green in a scuttle that took it four feet left of the flagstick. I failed on the birdie putt, the ball stalling short of the hole because of the same hurricane, but it was a marvel to see the forces of nature decide as fully in my favor as if they'd mistaken me for a pro who knew what he was doing.

I have dreams of such things. There have been times when I've put myself to sleep at night by walking a familiar course in my head, handling it shot by shot, scoring my birdies with flair and my pars with princely condescension. But there have also been pre-dawn wake-ups, when I knew there was nothing for me to do but really go out to a golf course.

Usually I was the first one there. The night would be grayly deteriorating, and first light would be a hint of orange just above the horizon. Walking with purpose, I could get through four holes before the sun was up, flaring over the white, dew-soaked fairways so that they seemed ornamented with jewels. Once I was joined by a German Shepherd, probably lost, and delighted to have company after a long night on the prowl. Racing after each ball I hit and then sitting with a hanging tongue until I finally caught up, the dog urged my speed to a higher level so that I finished 18 holes in an hour and a half and was strolling back to my car before the first greenskeeper arrived.

Evening, though, is my favorite time for golf. Eight p.m. in July and the sun behind a hill in the west, a full moon growing whiter in a wide, cobalt blue sky. Cinematographers call it the magic hour because of the softened texture of the light. The redness of afternoon is gone and colors seem enhanced by Kodachrome. Silky breezes cleanse and cool the air. Water sprinklers grandly shoot fountains over the fairways with a chicka-chicka-chicka, foosh! foosh! foosh! foosh! that takes you back to childhood and a quieter world where whole families sat on front porches and waved to passing cars. And as night falls and even an orange ball is hard to see, you hit into the far distance with faith that a green is there and your golf ball will find it, for that is how life ought to be and on such nights is.

# WHY I PLAY GOLF

A PSYCHOLOGICAL EXPERIMENT WAS ONCE PERFORMED ON HORSES. Each animal had been taught to stamp a hoof four times, say, when the trainer called out that number. The horses that got the number right were rewarded by a carrot or cube of sugar. But for experiment's sake, the trainers periodically denied the horses their rewards even though they had stamped as instructed. Confused and vexed by the mystery of denial, the horses became obsessed with counting out numbers with their hooves and could be heard clobbering their stable floors throughout the night.

So it is with golf. Even when I first seriously took up the game in my late thirties and was pretty much without a clue concerning the wild variety of contortions involved in a swing, golf occasionally and mysteriously rewarded me with soaring, dead center drives, high approach shots that danced ever nearer the hole, and putts that craftily wandered across the green and found the four-and-a-half inch cup as if the ball were a hound sniffing its way home. With seemingly the same swing, however, I could founder completely, the carrot or cube of sugar puzzlingly denied me. There would be times when my shot would be so wildly off-target that I could not follow its flight. If the golf ball had a voice it would have been shrieking. There's a lot of *What the heck?* on a golf course.

With rented clubs and my mother caddying for him, my father played his one and only round of golf in the 1930s. She seemed to have enjoyed the stroll, but he treated the subject of that afternoon with the stolid silence of soldiers who have witnessed the unspeakable in battle. He sensibly quit the game in disgust at that point.

Whereas I scored five eagles (two under par on a hole) in my first year of golf, a feat I have never since matched, and in the heroin of that rookie success I became addicted.

I hit my second hole-in-one between bouts of writing this. The hole was 177-yard par-three on the Coyote Hills course designed by Payne Stewart. I hit a soft as butter four-iron that sent my Titleist on a gorgeous, unerring trajectory over water to the front of the green, where it bounced once and rolled so unhesitatingly toward the pin it seemed to have a one-track mind. My golf buddy shouted with excitement, "That could go in!" And then it did, falling into the hole like a fat man finding a front row theater seat.

Rick told Ilsa, "We'll always have Paris," and that hole-in-one is my *Casablanca* moment. The highs in golf are hard to forget.

Mark Twain famously groused that golf was "a good walk spoiled," but it has become the favorite obsession of a great many other writers as various as P. G. Wodehouse, Harper Lee, John Updike, Tim O'Brien, Agatha Christie, and Cormac McCarthy. The focus golf requires and the bonhomie among playing partners that shared humiliation instills helps lock out the problems of literary craft as the writer instead concentrates on idle chat, ribaldry, the intense rehearsal of golf lessons, and the proper strategy for the next shot. Even sleep fails to empty my mind in such a helpful and restorative way.

It is a Zen-like sport that dictates very little muscular exertion, but a great deal of imagination, discipline, fine-motor control, and seemingly endless practice. Some hackers are foolishly proud of the fact that they've never had a lesson, whereas golf instructor Hank Haney recently told reporters that he was on hand for lessons with Tiger Woods for over one hundred days last year. And he hits six hundred balls a day, finding a groove that the muscles otherwise forget like freshmen do the rules of grammar. It's that hard to do well. So long as you get to position "A" at the strike, you can play the game with the low, scything swing of Lee Trevino or with the steep chops of amateurs who must be humming "I'm a lumberjack and I'm okay." But even a fractional mistake in alignment, timing, or clubface angle can result in a forest adventure or a cool dip in the lake.

Well-hit balls travel such a long way: a football field is just a wedge for me; my typical seven-iron shots could fly over the homerun fence in every baseball field in the world; the ho-hum drive of a professional carries the stunned, one-and-a-half ounce pill more than one-fifth of a mile. But John Daly too often demonstrates how being even a little off-kilter at impact can be ugly when multiplied by three hundred majestic yards.

But hundreds of golf club manufacturers are out there, laboring to correct our human frailties. I offer my humble thanks in the form of shocking cash outlays each year. They say a good carpenter never blames his tools, but Winston Churchill also griped that "Golf is a game whose aim is to hit a very small ball into a small hole with weapons singularly ill-designed for the purpose." And thus for many of us part of the allure of golf is the technological quest for the perfect equipment. Which means my lunch hours may be spent in a golf store waggling a six-iron to feel its heft, noting the mathematics of loft, lie, and bounce on some fancy new stroke-saver, trying out a gleaming new putter on a flat lawn of green carpet, or solemnly sorting through a used-club bin like young Arthur in search of Excalibur.

Renowned sportswriter Grantland Rice once put it that: "Golf is 20 percent mechanics and technique. The other 80 percent is philosophy, humor, tragedy, romance, melodrama, companionship, camaraderie, cussedness and conversation." You don't really play against an opponent in golf. You don't even play the course. You play yourself. The game unites the physical to those fundamentals of education, psychology, stamina, poise, and restraint that are already familiar to writers, and locates the examination of our qualities under the skies, in a vastness of green and wilderness, with four seasons of weather as our sometimes serene, sometimes truculent companion. There can be bliss at the end of a good day of writing, but mostly it's a grinding, flat-line activity that features the occupational hazards of anxiety, loneliness, punch-the-clock regularity, and sparingly parceled-out highs and lows. Whereas golf is a picaresque novel, its frequent tragedies enlisting the finest traits of the protagonist in countering the ills foisted upon him or her, but offering in compensation lucky bounces, surprising turns and encounters, flights of giddy, unearned success and, at least a few times each round, wondrous moments of elation.

# ACKNOWLEDGMENTS

THE AUTHOR WISHES TO THANK, IN ALPHABETICAL ORDER, THE PUBLI-cations in which these reflections first appeared: *America, Boston College Magazine, The Complete Roadside Guide to Nebraska, The Edge of Sadness, Evangelie Selon Marc, Image, Logos, Not Less Than Everything, Ploughshares, The San Jose Mercury News, Santa Clara Magazine, These United States,* and *Truthful Fictions.*

The author also wishes to thank Prairie Home Productions for permission given for quote written by Garrison Keillor for "A Prairie Home Companion."

This book was set in Arno Pro, designed by the American typographer, Robert Slimbach, for Adobe Systems. Named for the river that runs through Florence, Italy, Arno Pro is a contemporary adaptation of type styles that flourished at the height of the Renaissance Humanist movement.

This book was designed by Ian Creeger, Jim Tedrick, and Gregory Wolfe. It was published in hardcover, paperback, and electronic formats by Wipf and Stock Publishers, Eugene, Oregon.

CPSIA information can be obtained
at www.ICGtesting.com
Printed in the USA
LVHW012345040121
675751LV00007B/603